# Heresy

# Heresy

## HERETICAL TRUTH
## OR ORTHODOX
## ERROR?

A STUDY OF EARLY
CHRISTIAN HERESIES

JOAN O'GRADY

ELEMENT BOOKS

© Joan O'Grady 1985
First published in Great Britain 1985 by
Element Books Ltd
Longmead, Shaftesbury, Dorset

*All Rights Reserved*

ISBN 0 906540 75 5

Set in Bembo by Characters
Chard, Somerset

Printed by
Billings, Hylton Road, Worcester

Text and jacket design by
Humphrey Stone

*To Robert*

# CONTENTS

# INTRODUCTION

The ability to ask questions separates *homo sapiens* from the rest of the animal kingdom, and this ability is the foundation of his achievements. During a child's first years, 'why' is the most important word in its vocabulary and, if all goes well, will remain central there. In the process of learning, if the right question is put, knowledge can be gained. Every scientific discovery has been the result of a question being asked. Philosophies are formed by questioning what had previously been taken for granted and this type of questioning should also direct the study of history.

But it is not simple to identify and to formulate the questions that will unearth real problems; it is an art that has to be learnt by practice. The aim of this book is not to record facts, nor to give a detailed account of what early Christian doctrines and early heresies contained. It is an attempt, in the first place to ask the right questions, and then to follow where they lead; answering them is another matter.

It is almost impossible to imagine how history would have been without the existence of the world-religions – the religions of Hinduism, Buddhism, Judaism, Christianity and Islam – to imagine history without their genesis of cultures and civilisations, and of wars, division and strife.

This is particularly clear in the case of Europe. Try to conceive of European history up to the end of the Middle Ages without the history of Christianity. Most of it disappears – the greater part of our art, in the broadest sense, and most of the political and dynastic struggles, which form our national histories. The traditions and customs of Europe and its whole background of thought would have been quite other than what we know and much of what we consider good and what we consider bad, meaningless. Sad to say, some of the most brutal of Europe's wars might not have taken place had it not been for the existence of religion.

When any great system of ideas becomes public property, it tends to become distorted. But those of a very high order are doubly dangerous:

> Only ideas that shake the Universe
> Have power to be a blessing or a curse.
> For men will kill and torture for their creeds,
> 'Lilies that fester, smell far worse than weeds.'

People have distorted Christianity to such an extent that it has led them to act in direct contradiction to its fundamental principles. We can read about this in past eras and see it happening now. Because religious convictions have such emotional power, they can lead to more bitterness and hatred than anything else in the world.

Christians can argue about the propositions of their religion, in complete disagreement with each other – every person, every group tending to think they are right and everyone else wrong. And this has happened from the very beginning. But still the splits and splinters have not destroyed it, as well they might – have not turned it into a mere host of minor cults. Christianity has continued, despite all distortions and divisions, as a recognisable world religion. This is a remarkable phenomenon for which account must be given.

Christianity and Judaism are intrinsically related to, and rooted in, a particular area of the world and a particular time of history; in Christian teaching, Christ came to a specific place within a definite dated period – "He was crucified under Pontius Pilate."

The Jews of the Old Testament were a people whose history is recorded and known to us. Their records show that they felt a duty had been laid on them. This duty was to make known to surrounding nations that the Supreme Power was One and was Spirit. They had a historic mission. Later, the Christians used the Old Testament to show that Jewish prophetic writing and Jewish histories, real or allegorical, were pre-figuring the coming of Christ.

The existence of an institutional Church is closely connected with the historical side of Christianity. When it is taken as central to Christian belief that divine intervention came at a specific moment in earthly time and that human history had been leading up to this moment, it would make little sense for divine connection with human history to end at this point. Such a conception of Christianity necessitates a religion involved with the history of our world: therefore, integral to it would be the formation of an organised teaching Church, one of whose functions would be to continue to the end of time.

Christianity began in a relatively late historical period. Hinduism is many centuries, possibly thousands of years, older. It is without a Church or a set of definite dogmas, and yet it has continued without interruption and has unity. Hinduism "was not instituted but simply grew." (Hans Kung, *On being a Christian*) So it might seem that an institutional Church, with an established Creed, is *not* essential for continuation – Christians could have followed their founder's teaching and kept together without this. But Christianity appeared in a less ancient time and the date of its birth is all important. It may be that an organised Church was more necessary to the Western nature than to the East, which was and is much 'older' than the West. Among the nations where Christianity appeared changes were beginning to be more rapid, movements of people and, therefore, of ideas more fluid. Barbarism was approaching. For this era, for this region of the world, an organised institutional Church, with a recognised body of scripture and dogma, may have been necessary, if Christianity were to survive as a religious vehicle for mankind. Perhaps some form of 'orthodoxy' was essential.

Some maintain that this 'orthodoxy' was part of a Divine Plan, some that its development was due to the accidental results of men's words and actions. All that we can discover for certain, in looking back on what has been recorded, is that there existed in Palestine a collection of sayings and precepts, ascribed to an unknown teacher, together with an assembly of stories about him. With no general theory or system having been given, in a relatively short time a set of doctrines and rules of behaviour had been formed, which were understandable to a wide variety of nations and classes of people and which spread rapidly over the then known world. Even by the beginning of the second century the 'mainstream' body of Christian doctrine was forming and the 'Great Church' was recognised – to be either followed or attacked.

Every system of religion, philosophy, science or politics has its 'heretics'. There will always be those who, in their own opinion, are reformers of a corrupt system or are seeking a truer interpretation of it, but who are considered by the upholders of the system to be deviationists and distorters of what is right and true. Today, to be called a heretic is, in itself, considered something of a compliment – the description of an adventurous, independent thinker. But in the early centuries of Christianity, the term 'heretic' was one of grave abuse, and those termed 'heretics' would usually deny the appellation and would maintain that they and not their opponents were keeping the traditional line.

There can be no 'heresy' without 'orthodoxy', so, in looking at these early centuries, it is necessary to discover what 'orthodoxy' means and how certain teachings came to be included within it. Development of the original revelation was bound to take place; out of what was given, deductions would be made. As this development progressed some ideas came to be accepted, others rejected; some beliefs came to be regarded as true, others branded as 'heresies'.

The original meaning of the word 'heresy' was neither abusive nor complimentary. The word came from the Greek, *haerens,* meaning 'an act of choosing'; then, 'the course of action' or 'choice' – leading to 'the choice of philosophical principles' and to 'those who professed them', i.e. 'a school or sect'. Josephus, the first-century Jewish historian, used the term to mean a party or sect, without disparagement. Even St Paul, in *Acts* XXVI 5 used it in this sense: "that, after the most straitest sect, or heresy, of our religion, I lived a Pharisee." (Quoted in Cruden's *Concordance to the Old and New Testament*).

But in the epistles the word is used in a condemnatory sense. St Paul, in his letter to the Corinthians, said "I hear that there be divisions among you and I partly believe it. For there must also be heresies among you, that they which are approved may be made manifest among you." (I *Cor.* XI 18,19); and in the Epistle to Titus: "A man, that is an heretic, after the first and second admonition, reject, knowing that he that is such is subverted and sinneth, being condemned of himself." (*Titus* III 10). Such deviations arose even as the first Christian groups were being formed. In St Paul's writings they are condemned because he thought that they could change the whole meaning of the coming of Christ. But in the days immediately after Apostolic times, differing interpretations of the Christian revelation were not necessarily thought of as heresy. Doctrines were only in the process of formation.

Among the Church Fathers, Bishop Ignatius in the first century was the first to use the term 'heretic'. He used it against those who seemed to him to be confusing the true understanding of Christ. Then, as doctrinal formulation began to have increasing importance, the word 'heresy' came to mean 'any departure from the recognised creed'.

It was not until the great controversies of the fourth century that the derogatory meaning of the word 'heresy' became finally fixed – namely, as a 'doctrine maintained within the Church, but disruptive of its unity'. A 'schism' was an ecclesiastical cleavage, but a 'heresy' was a spiritual abberation (James Hastings *Encyclopaedia of Religion and Ethics*). By this time, many doctrines and dogmas had been formulated and had become the teaching of the Great Church – binding beliefs for those who belonged to it.

By the fourth century, the word 'heresy' had come to be used according to the present *Oxford English Dictionary* definition: 'Theological opinion or doctrine held in opposition to the "Catholic" or orthodox doctrine of the Christian Church'. It now included the yet stronger derogatory meaning of 'fundamental error, adhered to with obstinacy, after it (that error) has been defined and declared by the Church in an authoritative manner'. (Cruden's *Concordance to the Old and New Testaments*). The use of 'heresy' in this sense made it necessary for an 'orthodox' doctrine to have been defined.

To explore rejected beliefs and to discover how and why they were rejected is central to this book. In this exploration, only the great heresies of the first five centuries will be included. The reasons for limiting enquiry to this very early period are important.

Up to the second century the word 'catholic' meant 'worldwide'. By the end of that century it already meant holding to doctrines of Apostolic tradition as accepted by the universal federation of churches, which recognised one another. Rome, which claimed Peter and Paul as its founders, had long been accepted as the most important, and therefore the leader of these. By the end of the fifth century Pope Leo I had united in idea the Primacy of the Apostolic See with the Mission of the Roman Empire, (the Holy Roman Empire that was to be). The Great Church, with its centre at Rome, was now recognised as the Universal, or Catholic, Church; and what the Bishop of Rome declared to be 'orthodox' was 'orthodoxy'. Creed and Canon had been finally established. A present-day writer, describing Christianity as a religion among other world-religions, would find that, by the end of the fifth century, its basic tenets had been formed. His description of Christianity at that time would be similar to his description of Christianity today. It is in this sense, that the term 'mainstream Christianity' is used.

The early heresies were primarily concerned with doctrine. In the early centuries it was often due to the very heresies themselves that doctrines were formulated and re-formulated. Formulations were made in order to counteract or refute the heresy and this, in turn, led to further need for clarification. So the body of dogma requiring Christian assent continued to grow. The early heresies are important, not only because of their content, but because of their influence on doctrinal developments.

In mediaeval and later times most of the heresies centred on ecclesiastical and practical controversies or on the individual conscience against the established order. The connection of the Papacy and the Church with temporal government confuses the issue in a study of this kind. Politics came increasingly to colour the attacks on heretics and heresies; so that, in relation to the development of beliefs and doctrines, the later heresies are less relevant and less important.

From the time of the Reformation, Christendom has been divided. There are now innumerable sects and churches. The word 'heresy' is no longer used to describe the tenets of any particular Christian group. Nevertheless, there *is* a main-stream of Christian doctrine and it was in the first five centuries that it took its shape. The formation of 'orthodox' Christianity is clearly not a straightforward story. Some teachings entered the established creed and so formed the mainstream of Christianity; others became known as 'heresies' and created separate sects and churches, or else died out, either peacefully or violently.

The causes of this selection were many and its consequences manifold. Could this selection have been part of a divine plan, or was it the result of accident? Has the process of development continued in accordance with an ordained design, or, in that process, have there been deviations from an original, even an unknown, teaching? How much can we now discover?

Within this framework the early heresies will be explored and, in so doing, it is hoped that readers may be led to ask questions that they had not asked before.

# I

# THE BEGINNINGS AND
# THE FIRST DIVERGENCES

In the last half of the first century AD in a small corner of the
Roman Empire, groups of people were banding themselves
together to follow the instructions of men claiming to be
disciples of a teacher in Palestine. To most of their contemporaries they were yet another Jewish sect. To Romans in posi-
tions of authority, they were an extremely tiresome, and
possibly seditious one; and since, like all Jews, they would not
offer worship to the Emperor, nor worship the Roman Gods,
they were atheists. Followers, according to Tacitus, 'of a
pernicious superstition', they even worshipped their own
leader. As recorded in *Acts of the Apostles* written in 80 AD, "the
disciples were called Christians first in Antioch". By his adherents, Jesus of Nazareth was called Christ, the anointed one.
To the Romans, Chrestus was the name of a trouble-maker,
put to death in the reign of Tiberius. "Jews were driven out of
Rome for rioting at the instigation of one, Chrestus." (Sueto-
nius, *Life of Claudius*).

Today, with so many extraordinary cults proliferating
around us, it is not difficult to imagine how the first Christians
appeared to those around *them,* who now heard rumours of yet
another kind of religion, another sect. It is more difficult to
imagine how they actually saw themselves.

One of the weaknesses found in religious histories is that all
the adherents of a religion are assumed to be on the same level
of understanding. This is particularly apparent in the history
of the early Christian Church. For example, we are told that
the first Christians believed in the immanent, literal Second

Coming of their Lord – and clearly, from what we read, a great number did. But that does not mean that there were not others who understood differently or came to understand differently or expressed ideas with different meanings. It is probably safe to say that the more spiritual the understanding, the less widespread it is likely to be, and probably the less documented.

So one has to imagine groups of people who had themselves listened to the teacher in Palestine, or who had heard of his teachings through his disciples or through others – each interpreting what they had heard in different ways, and asking what this new religion was about. The most difficult question was (and would always be) who *was* this teacher, this Jesus of Nazareth? What manner of being was he? There were conflicting answers from the very first. This question is at the root of almost all the great heresies and any answer provokes more questions, which, in their turn, lead to further questions which can shape or create a form of belief.

The first Christians were of course Jews, and they continued their worship in the Temple, their reading of Jewish scriptures and their obedience to Jewish Law. At the same time, they followed Jesus as their master. But soon there was division. As recorded in *Acts* and in Saint Paul's epistles, there were distinct groups of Judaising Christians who insisted that Christian converts must keep the Jewish Levitical Laws and observances before they could be baptised.

There were divisions and uncertainties even among the apostles, themselves. At first, as has been said, the main body of the followers of the new religion were circumcised Jews, and the "gospel of the circumcision was unto Peter", (*Gal.* ii 7). St Paul was preaching to the Gentiles, the heathen. He wrote, "The gospel of the uncircumcised was committed unto me." (*Gal.* ii 7).

As stated in St Paul's Epistle to the Galatians, St Peter came to Antioch and lived and ate with the Gentiles. But the Judaisers from Jerusalem were so powerful that, when they came to Antioch, St Peter separated himself from the Gentiles, and

apparently insisted that they should "live as do the Jews." St
Paul "withstood him to the face." (*Gal.* II 11). It is recorded in
*Acts* that after dissension with "certain men that came down
from Judaea", Paul and Barnabas went up to Jerusalem to
settle the dispute by discussion with the "apostles and elders".
It was then decided that the Gentiles in Antioch and Syria need
not be circumcised nor keep the Law. They were required only
to abstain from meats offered to idols, "from blood, and from
things strangled, and from fornication". But the sect of strictly
practising Jewish Christians continued as a separate body
within the Christian community.

More fundamental than their insistence on Jewish obser-
vance was their belief that Christ was the greatest of prophets,
the expected Messiah, but that he was a man as other men.
These Judaising Christians became less important in the early
Church after the Fall of Jerusalem in 70 AD but from them
emerged a sect, the Ebionites, which was still in existence in
the fourth century.

From where we stand in history, after hearing for so long
the words and statements of Christian doctrine, we forget
how extraordinary they are. It is difficult to put ourselves into
the minds of those Christians near in time to the events that
gave birth to Christianity. For Jews, trained to centre their
whole faith on the conception of One God, it would naturally
seem blasphemous to conceive of Jesus as the Son of God.
What is amazing is that so many were able to do so, or at least
were able to believe that here was someone who was more
than a normal human being.

The Ebionites (the name probably meant 'the poor ones',
owing to their exaltation of ascetic poverty) thought of Jesus
as the Messiah, but rejected the belief in his divine nature.
They considered St Paul to be a heathen because of his teaching
that Jesus, a man, was Son of God. But, as time went on, there
were those among them who felt that they had to reconcile the
God-ordained status of a Messiah and the amazing deeds attributed to Jesus in the Gospel of Matthew (the only Gospel they

accepted) with the being of an ordinary man. Some held that
the Spirit of Christ – the anointed one – descended on the man,
Jesus, at his baptism by John, and left him at the crucifixion,
when he died – again as an ordinary man. This explanation of
the nature of Christ was to reappear later in various forms and
guises, not only in 'heretical' doctrines, but in the theological
controversies among Churchmen.

There were those who saw the question from the other side.
If Jesus was invoked as 'Lord' – the name for Jehovah – and
was 'come down from Heaven', then how could he be of
ordinary flesh and blood like the rest of us?

Some scholars say that Christ was not regarded as God until
well into the second century. But it was the practice of the first
groups of Christians, meeting for instruction and worship, to
offer prayers to God through Jesus Christ, and there was also
direct calling on the Lord Jesus in prayer. The *Didache,* or
*Teaching of the Twelve Apostles,* (probably written before 90
AD) describes this practice. And Pliny, a Roman historian of
the first century, says that Christians were singing hymns to
Christ as God. What then were they doing? Were they, as
Pliny thought, worshipping a man? If so, they would be
behaving in the same way as the pagan Romans.

For some, the answer was that Christ had only the appearance of a man on earth – he was, in fact, a phantom. Christ was
a Spirit, not a man. This line of thought became known as
Docetism, which is not the name of a heretical sect but a
tendency that was to appear in many schools of thought and
types of heresy in succeeding centuries. Docetism is found in
all systems which regard Christ primarily as a symbol, or as a
mythological explanation of man's relation to divinity. It is
said, (though it seems a tenuous inference), that in St John's
Epistles, there are warnings against those holding Docetic
beliefs, as for instance in *2 John* VII: "For many deceivers are
entered into the world, who confess not that Jesus Christ is
come in the flesh. This is a deceiver and an antichrist."

From the first, then, there existed two opposing conceptions:

Jesus, a man, although a great and divinely inspired one; and Christ, the pure Spirit of God, untramelled by humanity.

There were also the sceptics, like Celsus, a second-century Roman opponent of Christianity, who insisted that the idea of Jesus being a prophet or a divine Saviour was a gigantic hoax, spread by superstitious peasantry. How could the Eternal Principle become a man? For them, Jesus was either an imposter or else the fabrication of ignorant fishermen.

So who was he?

In the part of the world where this new religion began many races, nations and cultures met. The new beliefs had to be explained to a large variety of people. We hear of the poor and the downtrodden who flocked to the new revelation. But the elucidations and explanations, about which we read, were given to educated, sophisticated men – men interested in religious and philosophical ideas – thinkers and speculators.

There were the leaders of the Jews themselves, particularly the Pharisees, the strictest and most spiritually orientated of the orthodox Jews. For them, the importance attached to their history as a chosen people had to be included in a Christian philosophy of history. Their understanding of the unity of God had to be reconciled with a belief in the Incarnation.

There were Greeks, whose philosophy had brought them to the idea of one eternal principle underlying all things. To them the idea of Infinity entering into life on earth, or Pure Spirit being connected with materiality, was nonsensical and even horrifying. Among them were rationalist philosophers and sceptics, but there were also members of the Mystery Religions and initiates who had witnessed their secrets. There were those who had knowledge of oriental religions from Babylonia and Persia, and there were those learned in the studies and sciences of the Egyptians. Christian beliefs had to be defined so as to be understandable to all these questioners.

In the years immediately after the birth of Christianity there were no written records or written teaching. All that could be learnt about 'the amazing events in Judaea' was through oral instruction. St Paul's letters are the earliest written records about Christianity that we have. These letters were probably written between 50 AD and the year of Paul's death, about 64 AD. They had been collected and were being regularly read in all the churches by 90 AD. It is not known exactly when the three synoptic Gospels were *written,* but it is thought that they were circulating among the Christian communities soon after this and that the Gospel of St John was written at the close of the century. St Paul's letters, therefore, together with the Old Testament, were the first readings that the churches would have used.

In none of Paul's epistles does he give any stories from Jesus' life, nor any sayings or parables told by him, though he must have been familiar with the collections of Jesus' sayings and the reports of his deeds that were in existence then. It was, however, the relation of Christ to God, to man and to the universe that was important for Paul. It was this relationship that he wanted, above all, to explain to his converts. The two events in the Christian story upon which he dwells are the death and the resurrection of Christ. It is the spiritual and cosmological meaning behind these events that was at the centre of his teaching. St Paul was, in fact, the first Christian theologian – the first, to our knowledge, to develop a system from the facts and the teaching that had been given.

Even in Paul's lifetime there were those who reacted against what he taught; for example, the dissenting groups in Corinth and Galatia, which appear in the epistles. After his death many Judaeo-Christians in Antioch abandoned his teaching, considering it to be a mythologising of Christ and a purely mystical conception of Christ's role as Redeemer. Again, because of the development of his ideas, Paul has been accused, and notably by a school of writers at the end of the last century, of so changing Christianity as to become its 'second founder'. Nevertheless, the letters of St Paul were accepted, early in the second century, as authoritative Apostolic teaching, and so they have remained throughout the history of the Church.

Though in the epistles there are no references to details of Jesus' life and sayings, Paul probably thought that his readers were sufficiently conversant with them, through the oral teaching which they would certainly have been given. All those events and teachings were handed down primarily by oral transmission for many decades. This was still held to be the essential way for religious beliefs to be passed on to the next generation. As long as those who had been directly in touch with the apostles still lived, this method of spreading Christian teaching continued, together with written records.

Although many documents and writings were held sacred, treasured and read at the places of regular Christian meeting, it was the four Gospels, St Paul's letters, (excepting *Hebrews*), *Acts, I Peter* and *I John* that, early in the second century, received general acceptance as embodying the authentic Apostolic tradition. Other writings might be good and profitable to read. There was the *Shepherd of Hermas,* a description of visions calling to repentance, and, for some time, considered to be 'divine scripture'. There was the *Didache,* or *Teaching of the Twelve Apostles,* a manual of ethical teaching and church practices. There was a treatise called the *Letters of Barnabas,* which explained the Old Testament as allegory leading towards the New. And there were treasured letters from St Ignatius and St Polycarp. But although these were all considered holy books for private reading, they were gradually eliminated from use at public worship.

It seems that apart from the Gospels – then as now – the letters of St Paul and of some of the other apostles, and the description of the early Church and its life as given in *Acts,* were the only documents accepted as authoritative Apostolic writings.

Many 'records' of the life of Jesus were also available. They are even alluded to in *St Luke's Gospel.* (See *Luke* 1.1). Some became known as Apocryphal Gospels. The word 'Apocryphal' originally meant 'hidden or secret'; only later did it have the meaning of 'legendary', and therefore 'spurious'.

But the four Canonical Gospels, from their earliest appearance, were recognised by most (although not all) as something different, something self-authenticating. They were, at that time, accepted without question as having been written by those whose name they held. Later generations have queried this, and nothing can be known for certain of their authorship.

The aim of the Gospel writers was clearly not to present an historical biography, although there were certain historical facts given – possibly in order to anchor the accounts and the happenings to a definite time and place. Rumours of these happenings seem to have made small stir in the surrounding districts, in contrast to their later transforming effects. But whatever intepretation is or has been put upon these events, the New Testament writings, together with contemporary and near contemporary evidence, show that something took place at this actual moment which, then and there, gave birth to Christianity.

The documents which the first Christian communities used and which are now included in the Christian New Testament did not define in clear words exactly what *had* taken place. Different types of hearers were asking for an explanation and the first teachers of the new religion had to give them one. The first Christians themselves had varying conceptions as to the nature of their founder, and these sometimes conflicting conceptions had to be made understandable to people of different races, classes and cultures. There were problems, therefore, from the very beginning and it is by no means simple to discover how the mainstream of 'orthodox' belief emerged.

# II

# THE CLIMATE OF IDEAS
# AND GNOSTICISM

Early in the second century letters from venerated leaders and documents, often termed 'Memoirs of the Apostles', were being circulated. Using these records teachers began to gather groups of pupils around them. They taught these groups in their lodgings, as St Paul had done, or in the house of one of their followers. Classes were often held daily, usually in the early morning.

The original meaning of the Christian *ecclesia* (later to be translated as 'church') was 'assembly', deriving from the Athenian *ecclesia* meaning 'the assembly of citizens'. But the Christian *ecclesia,* in its first days, was, as St Paul termed it, the 'assembly of saints' because, once baptised, a Christian renounced the pagan life – not in theory, but in practice. This meant a truly heroic life, not only in the renunciation of all worldly pleasures, but in accepting possible martyrdom. For in the early centuries, before Constantine made Christianity a recognised religion of the Roman Empire, there were intermittent persecutions of Christians, some of horrifying brutality.

Two classes of students attended the groups: 'enquirers', who had not yet made up their minds to be baptised; and 'hearers', who had been accepted and who were undergoing preparation before baptism. This usually took three years and meant rigorous fasting, vigils and training in prayer. Those under training were the 'catechumens'. Even among them not a few hesitated before committing themselves to the heroic life, and remained catechumens for many years. As long as they

were catechumens, although they could partake in the
Christian worship, they were not admitted to the final part of
it, which led to and included the Holy Eucharist, the sacred
meal.

The teachers of the new ideas continued to exert great
influence. Catechumens and penitents gathered round them.
The atmosphere at the time was probably similar to that of our
own day. There was a general and pervading sense of dis-
illusion and of breakdown, so that many groups of people
were searching for a meaning in their crumbling world and for
deliverance from the troubles that they saw on all sides. Ideas
and systems of religion and philosophy were coming from the
East and from Greece and from Egypt, and meeting in this
active Middle Eastern centre. It must have been difficult then,
as it is certainly difficult now, to discriminate, and to discover
which teachings had true value amid the influx of pseudo-
wisdom, exaggeration and distortion. It was in this climate
that Christianity was spreading. Not only were local churches
being founded on the pattern set by St Paul, but different
schools, following different teachers, were growing up
amongst them, as had already happened at Corinth in St Paul's
time.

Among the teachers in these rapidly multiplying schools
were those later called 'Gnostics' by the Church Fathers of the
second and third centuries. What the Fathers termed 'Gnosticism' was considered by them to be one of the most dangerous of the 'heresies' which the 'orthodox' Church had to
face.

It is difficult, with the data that we have, to know exactly
what these gnostic teachings were. Until fairly recently our
knowledge of them came almost entirely from accounts and
descriptions given by the Church Fathers, who were attacking
them. Consequently, though the accounts of these systems
and beliefs sometimes seem to have been given with understanding, and are full and detailed, ridicule and hostility often
enter in, so that there must be an element of doubt in their

content. Most of the original Gnostic writings were purposely destroyed by the Church Fathers.

In 1945, at Nag Hammadi in the Nile Valley, a jar was discovered in a cave. This jar contained a whole library of Gnostic books, many from as early as the second century. They are Coptic translations from the original Greek or from Greek copies of the original, and appear to have been collected together in the years around 400 AD and buried for safe-keeping. They show that the refutations written by the Church Fathers in the second and third centuries – the source of almost all that had previously been known about the Gnostics – included remarkably fair and comprehensive accounts of Gnostic teachings.

The Nag Hammadi texts had been translated one by one into Coptic. The translator appears not always to have under-stood what he was translating. Unlike the Bible, where there are numerous texts to compare with each other, here there is only the one. So it is difficult for scholars to know what mistakes or alterations have been made.

Whatever truth there is in any religious system, it inevit-ably appears later in popularised and therefore distorted forms. Many of the Gnostic writings that are extant seem to show ideas that have degenerated. The documents found in the nineteenth century, such as the *Pistis Sophia*, date from the period of decadence, when the original ideas had become embedded in fantastic elaborations, difficult to disentangle. But, in the Nag Hammadi collection, there are certain writings of great depth, which bear the stamp of authen-ticity.

And yet there is a further difficulty. Many Gnostic ideas were purposely made obscure and hidden to keep them secret, so that much of what we read may not be understandable without some key.

There are dangers also inherent in the use of myth and allegorical forms. The second century Gnostics made great use of myth and personification of attributes and qualities. These can all too easily be taken literally and, even for those who originally understood them, the balance is difficult to keep.

All the great religions have their myths, as this may be the only way to describe what is beyond the confines of logical mind; but their use by a philosopher or teacher to explain a system often led to superstition and nonsense. "Only the highest type of mind, to which Plato belongs, can hold together the rational and imaginative in an organic way. At a lower level the pendulum swings." (C.H. Dodd, *Interpretation of the Fourth Gospel*).

Having read what is known about these systems there remain still greater problems. There were many different Gnostic sects in the early Christian centuries; basically they held the same main tenets, though some might be connected with Christianity and some definitely were not. But how much were their ideas based on more ancient religions or on contemporary religions coming from the East? How much were they part of a general system affecting all religions? Is what we know of them, even in their seemingly most profound form, a distortion of an older teaching which may have appeared in various forms in other times and in other places?

'Gnosticism' in its widest sense means the belief in salvation by knowledge – that is, by comprehension of the nature of reality. This, to the Gnostics, was comprehension of the soul's origin, its predicament in this world and the way out of the predicament. Such knowledge, they held, cannot be merely intellectual but must be experiential. It is primarily knowledge of the self – its true nature and its destiny. To explain this destiny various cosmogonies and cosmic systems were given, but always the aspiring soul had to travel upwards to its goal.

In many parts of the world – in Egypt, in Greece, in Babylon – we have accounts of mystery religions, which involve secret rites of initiation into various stages through which the believer must pass, often corresponding, on the cosmological scale to ascension through worlds or spheres in the universe.

In the forms in which these 'mystery cults' have come down to us, it appears that the reciting of certain secret formulae and the performance of ritual actions were supposed to ensure the soul's ascending passage. They almost certainly came to be understood in that way. But the Eleusinian Mysteries, teachings said to come from Pythagoras, cults from Persia and Babylon, accounts of the ancient Jewish sect of the Essenes and of the Ophites in Phrygia, all give hints and traces of the same understanding. This makes it seem possible that there were ideas in all of them that were of a different order from those of magic and superstition. In the writings of the second-century Gnostics, which the Church Fathers have recorded and which were discovered at Nag Hammadi, there occasionally seem to be connections of this same kind – connections also with the philosophy of Plato and with the Hermetic literature that came from Egypt.

"Nowhere do we find a pure form of Gnosticism; always it is built on earlier, pre-existing religions or their traditions." (H.T.W. Drivers, *The Origins of Gnosticism*). This may mean that the gnostic tendency apparent in the second and third centuries was a syncretic movement – the prevailing sense of instability at that time and in that part of the world leading seekers after certainty to select from all the religions that they could find anything which seemed appropriate to their own belief. One could say that the Theosophists have done the same in our own time. The Gnostics themselves held that revealed truth was witnessed in many religions; and that people who knew the truth would know the same truth. Certainly, the Nag Hammadi collection brought together various religious writings, not only of Christian and Jewish orientations, but also those seemingly based on Neo-Platonism and even Zoroastrianism.

Judaism, with its emphasis on history and obedience to the Law, would not seem to be a likely source for gnostic ideas; and yet there were sects within it which may have had some connection with them. The Essenes – 'the Pious Ones' – appear in the histories of Pliny the elder, of Josephus, the Jewish historian, and of Philo the Alexandrian – all of the first century. The sect was certainly in existence in the second century BC, at the time of the Maccabees, but its origin could have been much earlier. In these first-century accounts, Essene speculations on the nature of God appear to diverge widely from orthodox Judaism. "They were given to enquiry into the being of God and the creation of the Universe," Philo wrote. They studied the scriptures to discover their inner meaning, and used allegorical interpretations to explain them. God was the author of good alone, and the body mortal and transitory; the soul was immortal and of subtlest ether, lured by nature into the prison of the body. At death it was released and the divine spirit in man could then ascend through the spheres to its goal. There are hints here of what will be found later in the Gnostic teachings of the second century, but the Essene tenets were kept hidden and their rules of secrecy were extremely strict. That much we know from Josephus; but, though he lived in an Essene community for a short while, he was unlikely to have been sufficiently initiated to learn much about their secret doctrines. He tells of their strict organisation, their benevolence towards each other and to those around them and the asceticism of their life. He describes the grades in their society, their three-year novitiate before they could be accepted, the simplicity of their living and their goodness. But we cannot be certain that any of their writings are extant.

Pliny writes about a perennial colony of Essenes on the west shore of the Dead Sea. It is possible that the so-called 'Dead Sea Scrolls', discovered at Qmran in 1947 (and, many think, dating from before 70 AD) belonged to an Essene sect. The community who lived at Qmran at the beginning of the Christian era may have been Essenes or closely related to them. But these documents do not prove this, though rules of discipline are given and also descriptions of their rituals and forms of organisation. What can be discovered of their basic beliefs mainly concerns a struggle between light and darkness, good and evil, summed up in the battle between the Sons of Light and the Sons of Darkness, and between the two spirits governing man. "God made for man two spirits, that he (man) might walk in them till the appointed time of the visitation." These were the spirits of Truth and of Perversion.

There are detailed descriptions of the battles waged between the Sons of Light and the Sons of Darkness, but in the absence of any further explanations or earlier writings, it is impossible to know how much has allegorical meaning, how much is meant to be historical. We do not know who the 'Teacher of Righteousness' is, nor who the 'Wicked Priest', nor whether they existed historically at all. The Qmran documents may be related to Essene doctrines or they may have no real connection.

We can only know that, just before the birth of Christianity and during its early years, there were groups of people leading exclusive, ascetic lives, dedicated to spiritual achievement, and that they are likely to have had some influence on religious thinkers of the time. It has been said that the writers of the Gospels could once have been Essenes themselves – for Pharisees and Sadducees, the two other important Jewish sects, are mentioned continually in the Gospels and the Essenes, never. But there is nothing recorded to substantiate this possibility.

Alexandria, in the last centuries BC, had become a centre of Hellenism and of trade with the East. It was also the largest Jewish city in the world – a meeting-place for ideas of all kinds.

The Alexandrian Jewish philosopher, Philo, writing shortly after the birth of Christ, was the foremost representative of Hellenistic Judaism. His most important work was his *Allegorical Commentary on the Old Testament*. Philo was deeply influenced by Plato, particularly in his doctrine of God and creation. In Philo's exposition, God is indefinable, with no qualities that can be perceived by man. He is perfect Spirit and so cannot have contact with carnal substance. Through the mediation of Divine Ideas, or Forces, united into one Supreme force – the Logos – the orderly world came into being out of shapeless, lifeless matter. The Logos was the creative 'Word of God' in *Genesis* – the vice-regent of God.

Man's soul is a power of God, attracted into the sensual prison of the body. It can only attain freedom by resisting the allurement of the senses. Even in this life, man can acquire such virtue as to attain the Divine Vision, when the Spirit of God will dwell in him and "stir him like the strings of a musical instrument". For the wicked, this life is the real Hell. At death those who have lived free from attachment can return to their original condition with God. All others must, at death, pass into another body.

Many of these ideas will be met again in the teachings of the Gnostics, and it is possible that followers of Philo had formed sects and groups at the beginning of the Christian era. Their influence may have penetrated many circles.

In the centuries just before and just after the start of the Christian era, a body of literature was current in Egypt – the *Corpus Hermetica*. These tracts were written in the form of revelations from Hermes Trismegistus, ancient sage of Egypt, deified as Hermes, God of Wisdom, and, possibly, synonymous with the Egyptian God, Thoth. The oldest extant text is the *Poimandres*, and there also exist other texts, mainly in Greek, that were circulating in the second and third centuries AD in Egypt. All have the same outlook and religious basis, and many ideas in Hermetic literature are similar to some Gnostic themes.

In the Hermetica there is one God who is good and demands no service but virtue. Salvation can only be through knowledge – but this is knowledge *of* God, not *about* Him. To know Him is to be like Him.

Hermetic explanations of creation and of the position of the human soul in creation are found in many forms of Gnosticism. Primal Being (Mind, Light) created the universe, including seven planets, called 'Governors', who ruled the material world under the laws of destiny. Primal Mind also created Archetypal Man in His own image; Archetypal Man descended through the spheres and begot out of Nature, human-kind.

In the *Poimandres,* it is explained how the human soul can be saved from enslavement to the planets and can ascend through the seven spheres to heaven, whence came Archetypal Man. Knowledge is the key to unlock the gates and pass the Guardians.

"I, myself, Mind, dwell with the Holy and Good... I, myself, Mind, will not permit the assailing activities of the body to take effect. I am the guardian of the gates. But I am far removed from foolish, evil... and godless men." (*Poimandres* Treatise I).

"Ignorance of God is the greatest evil among men." (Treatise VII). Hermetic literature was not Christian in its form or terminology, but it had great influence on all the mystic and gnostic schools that were connected with early Christianity.

There was a sect, apparently in existence in Phrygia before St Paul journeyed there, known as the Ophites, taking their name from the serpent, which symbolised the rational aspect of the life principle. Their ideas had many similarities with those of the Hermetica. What is known about them comes almost entirely from attacks on them by the Church Fathers, Irenaeus and Hippolytus, in the second and third centuries. The Ophites had by then incorporated Christian terminology into their teaching and were treated by their attackers as heretics. As with other Gnostic sects it is difficult to know how much they were influenced by Christianity itself, and difficult to discover what is allegory and what is superstition in their system. Irenaeus and Hippolytus treated them as heretical Christian sects, as they did many other Gnostic groups.

The various sects enumerated by the Church Fathers differ from one another, but their ideas clearly have many important features in common. And it is these important features that must be considered in their relation to 'heresy' and 'orthodoxy'. The fact that there were ideas common to all Gnostic sects, which had affinity with those of other religious and philosophical systems, both ancient and contemporary, was either ignored or condemned by those who attacked

Gnosticism. Their anxiety to protect the Christian tradition, as they understood it, from any danger of disruption, forced them to disregard a powerful current of thought and belief, which might or might not have led Christian doctrine to develop in a slightly different direction from the one it actually took.

# III

# THE VALENTINIAN
# GNOSTICS

One of the fundamental questions in all religious systems and the centre of the many religious myths which attempt to answer the question, is the problem of Good and Evil. If there is an all-powerful and perfect Being, the originator of all things, how did error and misfortune enter into the Universe? Because, as we experience it, there patently *is* error and misfortune in our universe, the argument is often worked backwards from that fact, and the possible existence of an all-perfect Being is then denied. That, of course solves nothing either. The existence of biological order as against chaos has still to be accounted for, as, in fact, has the existence of anything. It is perhaps more difficult to prove that God is not, than that He is – more difficult to answer the question "how did goodness enter a mechanical world?" than the question "how did evil enter a consciously created one?"

In these first centuries of the Christian era the existence of a beneficent God, known by revelation or, as in the case of the Greek philosophers, of an all-perfect First Principle, discovered through metaphysical speculation, was the starting point of all cosmological systems. These basic assumptions being made, the inevitable questions are: where did evil come from and what was its relation to the good? How did perfection bring forth imperfection? How did the one changeless and eternal Reality bring forth the transient world of creation? Here lay the mystery of mysteries, seemingly beyond the scope of human reason, but for which every religion tries to give an explanation.

The knowledge – the 'gnosis', which gave the Gnostics their name – was the knowledge of this mystery of mysteries, and the essence of the Gnostic belief was that this knowledge was indeed beyond ordinary human reason. The Gnostics claimed that somebody had this knowledge and would give it to those human minds which could receive it – but only in the form of myth. How much the Gnostic systems of the second century were the result of their own speculative thinking and how much their interpretation of ancient traditions handed down to them, we do not know. But though the complicated myths which the Gnostics used to explain the existence of good and evil appear, at first sight, to be elaborate and fanciful extravagances, even the Church Fathers who attacked them accepted that a meaning lay beneath these elaborations. They treated most Gnostic schools as Christian, but as misguided and therefore harmful.

The greatest of the second-century Gnostic thinkers was Valentinus, who was teaching around the year 137 AD. He established schools in Egypt and Cyprus – schools which were still flourishing there in the fourth century – and then moved to Rome, where he held his most famous school. He never set up a church and has left no books of his teaching – though it is possible that the *Gospel of Truth*, discovered in Nag Hammadi, is largely his work. His pupils, the most famous being Ptolamaeus, carried on his school, and it was primarily against them that the Great Church's strongest apologist, Irenaeus, (Bishop of Lyons at the end of the second century), wrote his *Adversus Haeresis*. Hippolytus, ecclesiastical writer and presbyter of the Church at Rome, also attacked them in his *Philosophumenid*, written in about 230 AD. From these two, we learn most of what we know about Valentinus' teaching.

Valentinus thought of himself as a Christian. His aim was probably to formulate a Christian philosophy that would make Christian ideas intellectually acceptable to the Hellenised society of Egypt and Rome.

The Valentinian myths, which appear to us to be pagan and

polytheistic, were considered even by Irenaeus and Hippolytus to be metaphysical, and used to personify human qualities and abstract ideas.

Attempts to explain how evil entered the world have periodically been given in the form of a myth, representing a Cosmic Fall into error. In the Valentinian myth (and there were similar myths in other Gnostic systems) the Fall – unlike the story of Adam and Eve in *Genesis* – took place before the Creation of the world. The Old Testament Fall of Lucifer and his rebellious angels might be considered analagous, but there is a difference and this difference was one of the reasons why the Great Church considered the Gnostics to have turned their back on true Christianity. (The Gnostic schools broke with the main Church between 80 and 150 AD).

From Greek philosophy, from Eastern teaching, from Zoroastrian dualism came the Gnostic conception of matter as hostile to the good. This made yet more acute the problem, not only of how Perfection could bring forth Imperfection, but how it could in any way connect with it.

In Valentinus' system the Pre-beginning was termed Bythos – the Depth, boundless and unqualified, (cf. *Genesis* 1 1,2). Together with Bythos, Thought (the female principle) – also called Grace or Silence – produced Mind and Truth; and these four Principles or Powers are the root of all. From them came forth further Powers, known as Aeons. These were in pairs, male and female – active and passive principles. The thirtieth of these was called 'Sophia', the Desire for Wisdom. It was the error of Sophia that brought about the Fall and made our Universe.

Writings current at the time such as the Wisdom Literature of the Old Testament and the works of the writer, known as 'The Shepherd of Hermas', had accustomed people to the personification of qualities, so that myth was probably more easily acceptable to them than it is to us.

In the Valentinian myth Sophia fails to understand her limits and strives to return to the Father of All. This she cannot do.

She is prevented by Horus – the Boundary, the Cross. (In the *Acts of John*, one of the Gnostic Apocryphal gospels, is the phrase, "The real effective Cross is the marking off of all things.") In her grief Sophia gives birth to Ildebaoth, the shapeless one, from whom came our material world. The essence of this myth is that, though matter – the material of our world – is based on grief and ignorance, yet from the Mother, Sophia, came sparks of eternal, spiritual light and these are imprisoned within the material world.

Hostility between Matter and Spirit is a form of dualism, based on contradiction, which enters into many religious systems. This type of dualism had no part in Irenaeus' teaching. Much of his repudiation of Gnosticism is centred on the Christian principle, developed from the Old Testament, that God, the Creator, made a world that is good. "And God saw everything that He had made and, behold, it was very good." (*Gen.* 1 31). From that it follows that our bodies are also good.

It is in how they understood the conception of a Creator-God that the Gnostics departed most clearly from 'orthodoxy'. Nevertheless their conception would have been more intelligible to their Greek hearers than the one based on the Judaic Scriptures.

The Gnostics often equated the God of the Old Testament with the creator of our material world – for them a lesser Power than the Father of All. In Valentinus' system the Creator-God was limited by ignorance; in many other Gnostic systems he was actively malicious. But all the systems made a distinction between the Unknown and Unknowable Beginning and the lesser Power, who was responsible for the material world.

According to Valentinus, the Eternal Being, Originator of all, did not create a Universe from nothing, but contained all within Himself. He produced emanations, who in their turn produced emanations, spreading ever further from their source. Their ignorance of their source increased continuously as their distance from their Eternal Origin increased, so that error inevitably entered in and finally caused our world. The myth of Sophia's Fall was used to elaborate this teaching. In the *Gospel of Truth* there is the saying, "Ignorance of the Father brought terror and fear, so came error and made forgetfulness."

The idea of an ever increasing number of intermediaries between the Perfect, Changeless One and the multifarious world of material things bridged, for the Gnostic, the 'unbridgeable gulf' between Pure Spirit and Matter. And the conception of multiplying 'emanations', proceeding further and further from their origin, was the Gnostic answer to the question of how error entered the Universe.

Basilides, another Gnostic teacher, with a school in Alexandria, also taught the doctrine of 'Emanations' – the transmission of Life through intermediary beings to man. This never became Church teaching, but a descending hierarchy of Heavenly Powers was described by Dionysius the Areopagite, a mystic writer of the fifth century, and through him the idea entered into the spiritual writings of the Middle Ages. The origin of Basilides' system was probably connected with Zoroastrianism not Christianity. He is said to have written, "In the beginning there were Light and Darkness, which existed separately and were not made"; and that, in our world there is mainly Darkness, irradiated with some glimmer of Light. But in his description of the possible rescue of man from this Darkness there are traces of Christian teaching and Christian expressions are used.

Like the teaching of Basilides, the Valentinian system of cosmology was important only in its relation to the spiritual growth of Man. With the Fall of Sophia some seed of her divine origin – a spark of Light – was planted in Gnostic man. Therefore, his soul "cried to God for deliverance" from the prison of the inferior cosmos. The aim of 'those who know' was for this spark to return to its source, and the aim of Gnostic teaching was to show how to achieve this.

The Valentinian definition of Gnosis is "The redemption of

the inner spiritual man". The Gnostics 'know' that originally they were spiritual beings, but have now come to live in souls and bodies. Their aim is to be reborn into the spiritual world. Self-knowledge is the key. "He is a Gnostic because he knows by revelation who his true self is", (says a Gnostic writer in R.M. Grant, *Gnosticism and Early Christianity*). In his *Philosophumania*, Hippolytus quotes advice given by a certain Gnostic, Monoimus: "Abandon the search for God and the Creation . . . Look for him by taking yourself as the starting-point. Learn who it is who, within you, makes everything his own, and says 'My God, my mind, my thought, my soul, my body.' Learn the source of sorrow, joy, love, hate. Learn how it happens that one watches without willing, becomes angry without willing, rests without willing, loves without willing. If you carefully investigate these matters, you will find him in yourself."

In the teaching of Valentinus and in most Gnostic systems, a Redeemer had come from the heavenly realm to enlighten and deliver the immortal part of man, and to save him from being cast back into the sinful world after bodily death; because, from what we know of their writings, the Gnostics seem to have believed in cycles of rebirth. Salvation through a Redeemer, who came to earth and found his way back to the Father of All, in order to show the way, was the centre of Valentinus' Gnosticism. "He became a Way, a Gnosis, a Discovery and a Confirmation," (*Gospel of Truth*).

This deliverer, who was part of the vast Gnostic myth explaining the origin of the world and of Man, was named Jesus, 'the first mystery through whom all emanations flowed forth.' This 'aeon', Jesus, the summary of all the perfections of the God-head, descended into the womb of the Virgin and so entered into the body of the earthly Christos. Jesus thus had two persons – the psychic Christ, appearing as a man; and the in-dwelling Jesus, known only to the true Gnostic. "Material men were alien to Him and did not discover His appearance or recognise Him . . . The beloved Son, the embodied Word, came to reveal to the aeons the gnosis of the living Book – to teach, to suffer and to die. He taught in a school. False sages tested Him, but little children came to Him. At death, He divested Himself of these perishable rags, He clothed Himself in imperishability." (*Gospel of Truth*)

The Roman Christians at first accepted Valentinus as a legitimate teacher and he himself, it seems, did not want to break with the main body of the Church. But to the Church leaders his teaching was dangerous, chiefly because of his Gnostic conception of the being of Christ, which was similar to the Docetic doctrine that Jesus was not a man with a human body, but an 'appearance', a spiritual presence only; or, as Valentinus probably taught, his body was ethereal, of heavenly substance, totally different from our impure material bodies. The Gnostic idea of an ethereal Redeemer, descending from among the aeons through the spheres of the Universe, would turn the account of Christ's life into a mythological story. And if, as the Gnostics held, Matter were impure, God becoming man was an impossibility.

The Docetic tendency has appeared in different heresies throughout the ages; it even entered into the controversies between 'orthodox' Christian writers. The mystery of who Christ was has led to emphasis being laid sometimes on the divine character of Christ, sometimes on the human. In the Gospels, he himself asks, "Whom do men say that I am?" (*Mark* VIII 27). Many schools of Gnostics believed that the Heavenly Christ entered the man, Jesus, at the moment of his baptism by John and left him at the Crucifixion, when he returned to the Heavens from whence he came; or that at the Crucifixion, it was only a heavenly phantom who appeared to suffer and to die.

It is these two principles – the intrinsic evil of Matter and the mystical, as against the historical, conception of Christ which caused Gnosticism to be considered by the Church to be heretical, and dangerously so. But despite the fact that 'heretical' principles were attacked, the 'orthodox' teaching has never been completely clear on either point.

For many centuries the problem of reconciling the human and the divine nature of Christ caused bitter antagonism among Christians, from the scholarly to the humble. The very searchings and speculations of the Gnostic schools, judged heretical by the Great Church, became the main impetus in that Church's struggle to reach an exact definition of the relationship between the human and the Divine. In combating the Gnostic systems questions were raised that had to be answered. The fourth-century Bishop, Hilary, wrote in *De Trinitate,* "The error of others caused us to err in daring to embody in human terms truths which ought to be hidden in the silent veneration of the heart."

Perhaps the attempt to 'express the inexpressable' leads inevitably to conflict and so to 'heresy'.

The attempt to combat Gnosticism with definitions was to give rise to further definitions, and then to further arguments about these definitions, and so to accusations and counter-accusations of heresy. Irenaeus, himself, said that there are questions that are unanswerable and must be left in the hand of God. But once the questions were raised and other 'heretics' gave their response, it seemed that an official answer had to be given. It may have been necessary to have definitions, but it is possible that the very act of defining distorts the understanding of that which lies beyond logic.

That Matter, and so the material world, is of its nature evil is not Christian doctrine; but in Christian doctrine the conception of the evil of Matter has often become confused with the war against 'the flesh'. The conflict between 'flesh' and 'spirit' might appear in a less dualistic light if 'flesh' were understood, not just as 'the body', but as including everything that is not part of the search for God. But it was not generally seen in this light, and the old idea of the hostility of Matter has pervaded Christianity throughout the ages. It is connected with various forms of asceticism and has led to some exaggerated ascetic doctrines. On occasion, it has even turned what had been described as a religion of joy – the Good News – into one of grim severity.

This view of Matter is seen also in the ambivalent attitude of the Church towards sex and marriage. In many Gnostic sects, marriage, or the consummation of marriage, was forbidden, or forbidden to those of the greatest spiritual commitment. This was because of the Gnostic conception of the body as intrinsically evil. The Catholic Church did not hold this doctrine, and marriage became a sacrament. But though it was not until the late twelfth century that celibacy for the priesthood became a definite rule of the Catholic Church, the state of celibacy had long been considered to be of a higher order than that of marriage, and the ancient influence of Dualism has for many centuries caused the Church to look on sex with suspicion and even hostility.

The problem of Spirit's relation to Matter was interwoven with the problem of how evil entered into the world. This also remains one of the unanswered mysteries and, whatever myths are used to explain it, is a cause of conflict for many people. The complicated Gnostic myths were rejected by the Church and the myth of Adam's Fall accepted. The story of Adam came from the Old Testament, the original Scripture of the first Christians – the Scripture used to foretell the coming of Christ. But the Gnostic myth, describing emanations from the Godhead, multiplying and proceeding ever further from Him and therefore ever further into mechanicalness and ignorance, avoided the two great contradictions – an all-powerful perfect Being who consciously introduced evil into the Universe; or a first orginator who let evil in by mistake, and therefore was not all-powerful.

Both myths – the Old Testament and the Gnostic – implied the need for a Redeemer to rescue mankind from its fallen state. But the Gnostic myth, when popularised and taken literally, led to futile and incomprehensible elaborations; while the myth from *Genesis,* even when popularised and taken literally, was able to give some meaning to the Christian story. Nevertheless, the question of how evil and error entered a world created by a perfect, omniscient God is still a stumbling-block for many and, for many, has never been satisfactorily explained.

# IV

## GNOSTIC PRINCIPLES AND GNOSTIC LITERATURE

Central to the formation of a universal Christian doctrine is the question – how can a religion on such a high level be taught to, and made the rule of conduct for, the 'multitude'? By 'multitude' is meant not necessarily the poor and unlettered, but the great mass of those only superficially interested and with little spiritual understanding – often including 'the great ones' of the world. In the Gospels, Christ himself explained to the disciples, privately, teachings which the 'multitude' could only hear in parables. In the Gospels also, many of his sayings were said to be, for a time, beyond the understanding of the apostles themselves. How then could the Christian teachings that were handed down, and the principles underlying them that were formulated, expounded, and explained, be understood by the indiscriminate mass? There were geographical and cultural differences dividing the hearers of these doctrines, but the differences of level – spiritual and intellectual – would seem to present an even greater problem. "No great historical religion has wholly succeeded in bringing its message to the masses without making some concessions to the weakness of average humanity." (S. Angus, *Religious Quests of the Greek and Roman World*) A further question then arises – how great must these concessions be and how much do the concessions become distortions?

The Gnostics gave an answer to this question, though their type of answer came to be considered dangerously heretical by the Great Church. The Valentinian Gnostics held that people did not come into the world basically alike, but that there were three definite classes of human beings. There were the 'choics' – the earthly carnal ones, only concerned with the material world. There were the 'psychics', who lived by faith and good works – in fact, the ordinary Christian church-goers. And, thirdly, there were the 'pneumatics', the Gnostics, themselves, who had the Divine Spark in them and could ascend to their divine origin, because, according to the Gnostic myth, some seed of Sophia's divinity – Sophia, the Desire for Wisdom – was implanted in Gnostic Man.

The Redeemer came for the Gnostics and for those Psychics who could repent. In most Gnostic systems, the Psychics could never reach the height of the Pneumatics, and their heaven was that of a psychic Christ, 'seated at the right hand of the Creator-God'. In all systems the Gnostics could ascend with the true Christ to the First Beginnings. The Choics had no hope.

For those who held these beliefs, true, inner Christianity could be understood only by the one class of people, born on a higher level than the rest. Many could only receive it in a limited, exterior form, and the great mass could not receive it at all.

This doctrine of the three different levels of men seemed to do away with the difficulty of how Christianity could be explained to all people, regardless of their understanding. It seemed to take into account the many hard sayings in the Gospels. But though it solved some difficulties, it raised an even greater one. If men, from their birth, were divided into these categories, their destiny was already carved out for them. In many Gnostic systems, the Pneumatics were saved already, and in all, the lowest class was barred, from birth, from any possibility of growth. Only the Psychics had some choice, and that was limited.

The idea of a hierarchy among human beings has been, consciously or unconsciously, accepted until modern times. It gradually degenerated into an acceptance of social grades within society, and has now virtually disappeared in the West.

The concept of a class of men, by nature spiritually more advanced than others, was acceptable to the people of the first centuries. That some were born with an innate striving after Truth and would sacrifice all for this striving was clear to the Gnostics. "This is the manner of those who possess (something) from above of the immeasurable greatness, as they stretch out after the one alone, the perfect one, the one who is there for them." (*Gospel of Truth*)

According to many Gnostic teachers the essential purpose of these 'spiritual ones' was to strive upwards, so that through their efforts they could help others. For other Gnostic groups, these were already 'the perfect' and needed no salvation. This latter conception was to find its way into many later 'heresies', through the Middle Ages and beyond. As in so many religious teachings 'heretical' and 'orthodox', there may have been insights of value in Gnostic ideas, but these also held dangers when not fully understood, or when their balance was not kept. There was the continuous danger of the 'simple' exalting and venerating as 'perfect' those still far from perfection. For the 'perfect', there was the danger of Antinomism, which means literally 'the incompatability between two laws'.

Antinomism was not an 'heretical' system, but was, like Docetism, a tendency that appeared and reappeared in many schools and sects. It was based on the misunderstanding of an idea found in St Paul's epistles, (particularly in *Romans*), that those who lived by grace were beyond the Law. St Paul was teaching that when all thoughts and deeds are moved by the energy of God there can be no sin – the true Spirit within man does not sin. This was distorted to mean:- "It does not matter what carnal sins the 'perfect' commit; these are only in the 'natural' body and have no connection with the 'spiritual'."

In the original Gnostic conception it seems that the 'pneumatics' were not so much the privileged ones, as those from whom much more was demanded – much more than from the lower orders. "For, unto whomsoever much is given, of him shall be much required; and to whom men have committed much, of him they will ask the more" (*Luke* XII 48).

Today, the idea of different levels of humanity, as described by the Gnostics, would be anathema. Not only would it seem contrary to the idea of an all-loving God, but would go against all modern conceptions of 'democracy'. In the first centuries, it was not these objections that made this doctrine heretical, but the implicit denial of Free Will contained in it. It implied predestination.

Strangely enough, St Augustine, in the fourth century, one of the greatest of the Church Fathers, whose teaching was to be the most powerful influence in the Catholic Church for over a thousand years, was stronger in his ideas on predestination than the Gnostics ever were. The foreknowledge of an omnipotent God, on the one hand, and the consequences of Original Sin on the other were the foundations of his philosophy: from the beginning of the world, all that is to happen is already in the Mind of the Creator, and the fallen are unable of themselves to rectify the results of their sins. His refutation of Pelagianism – a heresy which will be discussed later – led him to the explicit formulation of these ideas.

The existence of a pre-ordained 'elect' was a central tenet of Gnosticism, though it never became part of Catholic dogma; yet the spiritual superiority of some souls over others appears to be an obvious fact. If there is a Divinely planned universe, this must be part of the plan. If this is so, how can it be reconciled with man's freedom of will?

The Gnostics made the problem less intractable for themselves by their belief in pre-birth – in a life of the soul before this life on earth. The true Gnostic 'knew' that he was a spiritual being, now imprisoned in a soul and body as a result of Sophia's Fall. Moreover, the Gnostics subscribed to a belief similar to that held in many Eastern religions – though they never clearly stated this – a belief in further lives after this one.

Some Gnostic schools held that there was a secret teaching given by Christ to his disciples and handed on by them to the chosen ones – the elect. Many of the Gnostic documents discovered at Nag Hammadi purport to be extracts from these secret teachings. Found at Nag Hammadi were the Apocryphon of John, and Apocalypses of James, of Paul and of Peter. These documents were in the form of dialogues between Jesus and the particular Apostle who was to hand on that secret teaching.

Some of the sayings in the Gnostic books seem artificial and contrived, as if trying to prove specific Gnostic theses. But there are others, particularly in the *Gospel of St Thomas*, that are not like this. The fragments of this 'Gospel' found at Nag Hammadi have been dated about 400 AD; it is the most complete Apocryphal gospel that we have. It is written in the Coptic language and was presumably translated from an earlier Greek original, thought to be of the second century. Some scholars believe that it is closely related to St Mark's Gospel, assumed by many to be the main source, or based on the main source, of the Synoptic Gospels.

The Gnostics called the *Gospel of Thomas* the *Secret Sayings of Jesus*. The preface to this gospel reads: "These are the secret words which Jesus, the Living, spoke and which Didymus Judas Thomas wrote. And He said: He who will find the interpretation of these words will not taste death." (Quoted by R.M. Grant in *The Secret Sayings of Jesus*) In the Gospel of Thomas, 'to understand' is equivalent to 'keeping the word of Jesus'.

The *Gospel of Thomas* had disappeared and was not discovered until 1945, and then only in its Coptic translation. But Bishop Hippolytus mentioned it in the third century, saying that it was used as their sacred book by the Naassenes, a second-century Gnostic sect, whose doctrines, as described by Hippolytus, seem to be closely related to the teaching of 'Thomas'.

The Naassenes were a branch of the Ophites and, like them, they revered the snake as the symbol of wisdom. They may

even have identified this symbol with Christ. As with all
Gnostic schools, they believed that Christ came to reveal
saving knowledge to chosen disciples and that traces of their
gnosis could be found in ancient traditions – in the Jewish
Scriptures and even in Oriental religious teachings.

They believed – and their beliefs were similar to those found
in Egyptian Hermetic literature – that the Primal Being was
three-fold, spiritual, psychic and material, and that all three
elements formed Archetypal Man, who descended to earth
and begot human nature. All three elements entered into Jesus
and worked through him. Humanity consisted of three types,
as all Gnostics believed. The different grades of humanity in
the Naassene system were also akin to those described by the
Gnostics. There were the 'gnostics', the 'psychics' and the
'choics'; and so there were three types of 'church' – 'the elect'
(the gnostic), 'the called' (probably the Christian churches of
the time) and 'the captive' (which would be for the rest of
humanity). The 'gnostics' were those who were able to receive
and understand the saving knowledge.

The main theme of the Sayings collected in the *Gospel of
Thomas* is that true religious experience is the recognition of
one's own identity. "When you know yourselves, then you
will be known; and you will know that you are the sons of the
Living Father. But if you do not know yourselves, then you
are in poverty and you are poverty." (Quoted by R.M. Grant
in *Secret Sayings of Jesus*).

The collectors of the *Secret Sayings* probably claimed, not
only that many of these Sayings were unknown to the Christian churches, but that the Canonical Gospels, as read in the
churches, were merely 'psychic teaching' and should be interpreted by those who knew the secret tradition. *The Gospel of
Thomas* was such an interpretation.

In the *Gospel of Thomas,* it is the inner meanings of Jesus'
Sayings that alone have importance. The Kingdom of Heaven
is never seen as a consummation to be looked for in the future,
but exclusively as a state *within* a man – in fact, the state of self-

knowledge. There is no mention of the Resurrection, and the idea of resurrection is given in purely spiritual terms – "Come into Being as you pass away." Human existence is not true being; true being is only achieved when human existence is transcended. Salvation was not seen as an act of God nor as something that could take place in the future, but as the present acquisition of knowledge. Knowledge of where a man comes from, who he is, and where he is going is the kernel of Gnosticism. This knowledge is not given by intellectual in-struction, but it is the possession of a special revelation for those capable of receiving it. The Gnostic attitude to Christian tradition, therefore, necessarily implied the handing down of secret teaching to an inner group – to people with developed understanding.

The *Gospel of Truth,* which was mentioned in the writings of Irenaeus and Hippolytus but which has only recently been discovered among the Nag Hammadi documents, does not pretend to give the words of Jesus himself, but is about him and about the theme, central to Gnosticism – "If one has knowledge, he is from above . . . Having knowledge, he does the will of the one who called him . . . He who is to have knowledge in this manner knows where he comes from and where he is going."

Irenaeus did not explicitly reject this 'Gospel'; he said only that it was unlike the other four. But the 'orthodox' Church never accepted into its teaching the existence of a chosen grade of believers, and Irenaeus affirmed that there could be no hidden teaching, or else the successors of the apostles would have spoken of it.

By the end of the second century, the accepted Canon of Scripture was more or less as we know it now. It is not difficult to see why what was accepted was accepted. It is more difficult to understand why some documents were left out. There was a *Gospel of the Hebrews* mentioned by Jerome, theologian of the third century and by other ecclesiastical writers of the time. Sayings of Jesus were sometimes quoted by them from a source now unknown to us. One of these, ascribed to Jesus though appearing in no known Gospel, is this teaching on prayer: "Ask for the great things and God will add unto you the little things" (Quoted by Maurice Wiles, *The Making of Christian Doctrine*). Some of the Gnostic 'gospels' were also in circulation at this time. In the late nineteenth century, fragments of a Gospel of Peter were discovered in Upper Egypt. Eusebius, an 'orthodox' Church historian of the fourth century, had mentioned it, saying that in the year 190 there were queries about the Gospel of Peter and that it was rejected by the Church leaders as giving an unreal and mythological picture of Jesus.

What was agreed to be Apostolic authorship became the test for inclusion in the Canon of Scripture. It is probable that fear of Gnostic heresy excluded all writings that seemed tinged with it. The Apocryphal gospels portrayed Jesus as the Divine principle, the totality of authentic being, but *not* as a human being, living a human life at a definite period of time. So one reason for the rejection of these gospels may have been that they had no connection with historical fact. Historical reliability was considered to be an essential ingredient of 'orthodox' Christian teaching.

The fear of Gnosticism even brought the Fourth Gospel under suspicion. "You shall know the Truth and the Truth will make you free" (*John* VIII 32), was thought by some Gnostic schools to sum up their whole system; and the first fourteen verses of St John's Gospel would also be especially relevant for them. Nevertheless the four New Testament Gospels had secured acceptance very early and there was never serious doubt about them as the kernel of Christian Scripture.

That there was a secret teaching given orally to chosen and specially ordained pupils cannot, of course, be disproved, though the existence of such a teaching was strongly denied by the Great Church; and, in like manner, there is no proof that it ever existed. But belief in the possibility of such a teaching

entered into many of the early Christian heresies and unortho-
dox schools of thought, and is one of the reasons why the early
heresies are especially important in studying the development
of Christianity. If this 'heretical' belief is true, then Christianity, as it developed, may well have deviated from that
original, but largely unknown, source; and if this be so, was
the deviation by accident or design? These are the questions
with which this book opened, and out of which further questions may grow.

# V

## THE TWO ALEXANDRIAN
## TEACHERS

It will soon appear that more space is being given to discussion
of the Gnostic than to any of the other heresies. This is because
it was regarded, at the time, as the most serious of all the
threats to the existence of a unified and catholic Church, and it
therefore needs the most elaboration. Gnosticism also contains
within it ideas important for later times. Gnostic tendencies
reappear in later heresies, especially in those of the late Middle
Ages. They appear in some religious groups today – for
example, in certain groups formed for meditation, or for the
achievement of greater spiritual consciousness, both within
and without the mainstream churches.

The central aim of the second-century teachers of Gnosticism was to establish an understandable Christian philosophy
and a system to live by. The fourth-century controversialists,
on the other hand, were concerned with refutation of error in
points of doctrine, and the fourth and fifth-century heresies
arose out of the exploration or defence of such points. These
controversies were of more fundamental importance than
sometimes might appear, but, nevertheless, their argument
was basically an intellectual one of definition. Those who
belonged to and those who attacked the Gnostic schools were
concerned to discover what Christianity *was;* for above all, the
Gnostic heresies were spreading at a time when Christian doctrines and modes of worship were still in a state of formation.

These early heresies, from what we can find out about them,
would seem to exemplify the most interesting elements in all
'great heresies' – that is to say, the teaching may have

contained an idea of great value, but the *teacher* may have expounded it before he had attained sufficient stature himself fully to comprehend it; or the teaching may have fallen into the wrong hands and so become distorted or trivialised; or it may have lost its balance through over-emphasis. Hints of all these things can be found in the discovered records of the Gnostic sects.

But there is more to it than this. The question has already arisen – how much has been lost in condemning the Gnostic schools and in turning away from them? It is here that the study of Gnosticism is important, because this is a question that cannot be ignored and must be constantly returned to.

Clement of Alexandria and Origen – Christian theologians of the second and the beginning of the third centuries – did not reject all Gnostic ideas. Clement of Alexandria (c. 150 to 215 AD), Presbyter and head of the Christian catechetical school in that city, often quoted from the Gnostics. He considered Valentinus and his school to be Christians bent on finding the truth, though led into error by misunderstanding Greek and pagan philosophies.

Origen, (c.185 – c.254) was Clement's successor as Presbyter of the school. Both he and Clement had much in common and much sympathy with the Gnostics, especially with the Valentinians; but the Alexandrians' views, though influential, were not incorporated into 'orthodoxy', and several of Origen's ideas were actually condemned as heretical in Councils of the fifth and sixth centuries.

Clement, the 'blessed presbyter', as he was called, was revered by all early Christian writers as a truly saintly man. He was acknowledged as a Saint of the Church until the eighteenth-century Pope, Benedict XIV, having read and believed a hostile account of Clement's work by Photius, a ninth-century ecclesiastical writer, excluded Clement's name from the catalogue of Saints. This was, and is, regretted by many.

Clement's ideal was the Christian Gnostic. "The true gnostic is the Lord's brother and friend and son," he wrote in his

*Stromateis* (meaning 'miscellaneous collection' – literally, 'bag of oddments'). And he even went so far as to say, "The gnostic practises being God, and has already become God". (*Strom* IV 23). Like the Valentinians, he did not equate the saving knowledge, necessary for perfection, with intellectual enquiry, though he felt strongly that reason had an important part to play.

In Clement's teaching, true experiential knowledge comes through the continued practice of faith and love. He disagreed with the Gnostic conception of the world as evil. But anything which he thought to be of value in the Gnostic systems Clement accepted and made use of, just as he made use of Greek philosophy, which he held to be the forerunner of Christianity, for him the highest exposition of truth. In fact, for Clement, Christianity was essentially a philosophy in its original sense of 'love of wisdom' – a search for wisdom and the true way to gain holiness (wholeness).

Clement wrote that Truth is Truth wherever it is found, and it is everywhere the word of God. "It is the unique Word, which has given out to each nation, through the angel set over it, the form of wisdom proper to it. Wisdom is one in principle but multi-form in presentation. This same Word manifests itself anew in Christ, but the same pattern remains," (as quoted in Daniélou and Marrou, *The Christian Centuries – The First Six Hundred Years*). Clement was never formally attacked for his ideas, but they seem to have been forgotten and set aside.

Christ, as Clement taught, was essentially a teacher and a revealer, who came to lead men, through wisdom, to become Sons of God. Like the Gnostics, he thought that there were grades of Christians. There were the 'pistes', who accepted Christ without knowing why and who worked only in obedience and for a hoped-for reward. These formed the great body of the baptised. There were also the 'pneumatics', who had some knowledge in addition to this and knew what they were doing. But, unlike the Gnostics, in Clement's doctrines, there was a possibility for everyone who worked towards the true practice of contemplation and right living to progress and so to become a true gnostic and attain fulfilment.

One can find in Clement's writings the assumption of a secret Apostolic tradition – an allegorical teaching, handed down, not through a succession of bishops but of teachers. Clement wrote that "after the resurrection, the Lord delivered the Gnosis to James the Just and to John and Peter; they delivered it to the other apostles", (from Eusebius' *Church History* 2, i.4). There must exist, if this be so, an esoteric as well as an exoteric Christianity.

This idea was more clearly expressed by Origen, who had listened as a boy to Clement's lectures. Origen, as well as being a committed and devout Christian and Christian traditionalist, was a philosopher who had studied the Gnostic systems and who clearly knew a great deal about the Gnostic schools that existed in his time. He held that man was striving towards a sorrowless condition – a state of order and of rest. This could be reached by intense practice of contemplation and by self-knowledge, which, for him, meant Divine Wisdom. "The soul is trained, as it were, to behold itself in a mirror. It shows the divine spirit, if it should be found worthy of such fellowship, as in a mirror, and this discovers traces of a secret path to participation in the divine nature."

But Origen accepted that complete and certain knowledge rests wholly on Divine Revelation. This means that he desired his cosmological speculations to be based on the sacred Scriptures, whose understanding had a special significance for him. In his teaching the facts recorded in the Old and New Testaments appear as vehicles of ideas, and their importance lies in this aspect. Unlike the Gnostics, Origen emphasised the empirical and historical in Scripture, as concrete facts. But for him their actuality did not give them their value; historical Christianity was the husk which enclosed the true kernel.

What was fundamental in Origen's exposition of Christianity was his insistence that scriptural ideas existed on three different levels – the 'Flesh of Scripture' was the body of happenings in time and space, which was to edify the masses; the more advanced, the 'pneumatics', could study the mysteries, the 'Soul of Scripture'; only the 'perfect' could understand the 'Spirit of Scripture' – the level above mere history. Certain Christian teachings, he said, should not lightly be committed to writing; without the 'key to knowledge' there would always be mistakes in the teaching of Scripture and Christian Tradition.

Origen's view that the recorded facts of Christianity were of small value beside their secret inner meaning was difficult to reconcile with the rules of faith given to the congregations in the churches. And it was on this point that Origen made clear his belief that there was both an esoteric and an exoteric Christianity.

Although the Christian masses could not grasp the deeper meanings expounded in the Scriptures, the 'flesh' of Scripture was necessary for their life and growth. Simple faith was enough for Salvation, and the Church had embodied the substance of Christian belief in its exoteric rules of faith. Anthropomorphic language was what could be generally understood, but Christ would have different meanings according to the believer's spiritual progress.

The centre of Christianity for Origen was Christ; not as Man, but as Logos – the Logos who was with the Father from all eternity. Those who had striven to draw near to the Logos – men such as Socrates and Heraclitus – were Christians before the coming of Christ.

Some Gnostics had incorporated Jesus into their cosmological scheme – he was the mythical Revealer, who came from above. His descent from Heaven, and his ascent back to Heaven were symbols of the soul's destiny. Christ was the Archetypal Man. Origen had sympathy with the Gnostics' views, but he did not agree with them that all the facts stated in the Christian Revelation were purely symbols of the inner life. Christianity, he said, was a practical principle, unfolded in

historically revealed facts. Nevertheless, he taught a cosmological and theological system that incorporated many ideas
not found in the traditional Christian teaching of the time.

In Origen's system the first act by the Father of All Being
was to create the realm of intelligences. Some of these spirits
cooled in their love for their Creator and fell away. God made
the material world as a means of recovering these spiritual
beings who, through their own fault, were now imprisoned in
human bodies.

Origen believed in a pre-mundane fall, as did the Gnostics,
but, unlike the Gnostics, he believed that the Creator God was
good and all-merciful, creating the world as a training-ground
for human souls, which the fallen spirits had now become, so
that they might return to the Fount of their Being. The
'world', unlike the Gnostics' 'world', was not evil – the suffering in it being necessary for the training and purification of the
fallen souls. For him, evil's root was purposelessness – absence
of good – and God did not punish. The punishment of human
kind consisted in their turning away from where alone true
happiness could be found. Their redemption consisted in
being shown the way to find it again.

Depending on the quality of their life on earth, souls might
evolve or degenerate. After further lives of striving, finally, *all*
would be saved. This last belief was contrary to that of the
Gnostics, who assumed a pre-destined elect. Origen believed
that every man has within him the image of the Divine Word.
Unless he destroys this entirely, there is always hope for him.
He believed in the possibility of attaining perfection after
death. The soul's growth in comprehension would continue
through a slow and painful ascent of many lives. As no one on
this earth is sinless, there will be purging 'fire' at death. This
belief in the restitution of all souls back to purity and blessedness, through the means of suffering, contained within it the
germ of the doctrine of Purgatory. And the idea of Purgatory
became a general assumption in Church teaching from then
on, though it was not formulated till Gregory the Great did so

in the sixth century, and it was not included in official doctrine until the thirteenth. Yet the final restitution of all things was, in Origen's teaching, relative, since all spirits inherently possess free will and so could fall again. God remains eternally immutable, but the falling and the rising may continue. Origen did not conceive the End as an apocalyptic transfiguration of the world, but, as in Gnostic doctrine, a liberation of the spirit from its union with the sensual. His was a spiritual, not a physical resurrection.

Origen taught that the idea of three persons within the Godhead was fundamental to Christian understanding – the Father, unbegotten and immutable; the Holy Spirit, brought into being by the Father through Christ, the Word; and the Word, the Logos, continually begotten by the Father. The Logos is the wisdom and power of God, directing the Universe. So the Word is midway between the Uncreated God and created things. But, though in the way in which he wrote the Son appeared subordinate to the Father, Origen held that the immutability, the pure knowledge and the blessedness of the Father were communicable attributes, and so the Son possessed complete Divinity.

Origen's teaching influenced many Christian thinkers, but some of his ideas were held to be heretical, and the Council of Alexandria in 400 and that of Constantinople in 543 condemned them. Strangely enough, Origen was not attacked for the general scheme of ideas that formed his system, though they might have been thought to be close to Gnosticism and to be a departure from mainstream Christianity; for example, what would appear contrary to the teaching of the Great Church was the distinction which he made between the ordinary 'pistis' (the piety of the 'faithful') and special spiritual 'gnosis' – in fact, the existence of 'two Christianities'; and indeed his whole conception of man's redemption – the fallen spirits returning through many lives to the source of their pure being – might have been expected to be equally unacceptable. Instead, he was attacked on isolated propositions, such as his conception of a spiritual as against a physical resurrection. His belief in the pre-existence of souls was said to be heretical, and his teaching on the restoration of all things back to God was attacked on the grounds that this must include even the devils. Above all, he was accused of heresy on account of his exposition of the Logos and of the explanation which he gave of the Son's relationship to the Father. He was accused of making the Son subordinate and so detracting from His Divinity. And yet, in the religious controversies concerning this relationship, both sides drew most of their ideas from him.

In the same way as Clement, Origen recognised what was of value in Gnostic teaching and developed it, though, strangely enough, much of what can now be learnt of his ideas comes from his writings against what he held to be Gnostic errors. For both Clement and Origen, there existed a question that has never been answered – was there an authentic tradition, unknown to the ordinary Christian, on which the Gnostic writers relied?

It is ironic that a great part of Origen's teaching should have been obscured by theological argument and controversy, because, for Origen, Christianity was essentially not a doctrine, but a life; not a Law, but a Spirit. He laid special emphasis on the importance of the Spirit as against the Letter in all Christian teaching. And yet the creation of a permanent, institutional Church demanded the 'Letter'. Already, Irenaeus, the great second-century apologist, had begun to propound what the 'Letter' entailed.

Irenaeus, Bishop of Lyons, lived between c.130 and 202 A D. Up till that time the word 'catholic' meant simply 'worldwide'. By the end of the second century, it meant holding to doctrines of Apostolic Tradition as accepted by a universal federation of churches which recognised one another.

Irenaeus' main concerns were to preserve what he held to be the Apostolic Tradition, and to ensure that every church agreed with the Roman Church as a matter of necessity; for, he said, this Church represented the leadership of faith. "And to this Church, on account of its more powerful leadership, it is necessary for every church to gather; that is to say, the faithful from all quarters, because the tradition from the Apostles is preserved there by those who come from all quarters." (*Adversus Haereses* III 3 1).

Irenaeus' great work in five books was entitled *Against Heresies*. The use of the word 'heresy' in a work which received general acclaim shows that, already by the second century, there was a collection of belief that was considered to be 'orthodox'.

The main object of Irenaeus' attack was Gnosticism. He considered, as did Hippolytus and Justin Martyr – also writing in the second century – that Simon Magus was the founder of Gnosticism; and they equated a Simon, (possibly a leader of a Samaritan sect that had spread to Syria, Phrygia and even to Rome) with the Simon of *Acts* VIII. "But there was a certain man, called Simon, which before time, in the same city, used sorcery and bewitched the people of Samaria, giving out that himself was some great one; to whom they gave heed from the least to the greatest, saying 'this man is the great power of God'." Hippolytus attributed a 'gnostic' book called *The Great Revelation* to this Simon.

As in all Gnostic sects, the 'Simonians' held, as one of their central beliefs, that within humanity, or within some portion of humanity, a Divine Spark was imprisoned and this had to be redeemed. Irenaeus maintained that Simon, the leader, announced himself as this Redeemer – the Supreme God, who had descended through the worlds to appear as man (though not a man) in order to set right that which had gone astray on earth. In this form the belief naturally appeared blasphemous to Irenaeus, but he was also attacking the general Gnostic idea of a mythical Saviour (using 'myth' in its sense of a philosophic abstraction or cosmic explanation); and he opposed this Docetic interpretation of Christ – that is Christ as purely a spirit-being. An essential element in Irenaeus' teaching and in what became 'mainstream' or 'orthodox' Christianity was the belief that Jesus Christ lived on earth as a human being in historical time. Irenaeus held that only in this way could Christ recapitulate perfection step by step, thereby showing that mankind had the possibility of a return to the immortality lost by Adam's fall. God created man in His image to live in a world created for his use and for his training.

It was the speculative, subjective and unhistorical approach of the Gnostics that Irenaeus found dangerous – especially because it could lead, and in fact did lead, to a proliferation of schools and of 'gospels'. It was a single teaching, handed down from the Apostles and their successors which Irenaeus was concerned to establish and preserve. As a boy he had listened to St Polycarp; and St Polycarp had been a disciple of St John. He felt, therefore, that he could personally witness to a continuity of teaching.

Irenaeus maintained that there was an oral tradition given by the Apostles to the Elders and, from them, to the bishops whom they appointed, and so on to their successors. The four Gospels were the written records of this teaching in four forms. Matthew, he thought, was the first to write. But it was not the Gospels that Irenaeus held to be the primary authority, but the voice of the succession of Elders; and the original *kerygma,* or oral teaching, which was later written down in the Gospels, had been possessed by the Apostles in its entirety. Irenaeus insisted that if they had known of hidden mysteries, they would have told their successors.

Questions had arisen and different interpretations had been given from the very beginning of the new religion. Irenaeus does not enter into this, but writes in order to show that a teaching had continued without a break, and that its reliability was guaranteed by an unbroken succession of authority. To prove this, he traced a continuous line of Bishops of Rome back to St Peter, himself the first Bishop of Rome. Irenaeus gave the Bishops of Rome as the example of a continuous succession of authority, because he held Rome to be the pre-eminent and leading church. He believed this to be so because tradition held that the Roman church was founded by St Peter and St Paul, both martyred in Rome. And because, as he said, "all roads lead to Rome", it was possible for interpretations of Christian teachings to be checked there in the one centre, and the true character of the universal faith could thus be clarified.

The Gnostics, too, put their faith in an oral tradition, but they maintained that it was a secret one, given only to those who could understand; and they suggested that the apostles themselves often did not understand it. Even in the next generation, they said, the purity of the teaching was no longer perfect. Hints of a 'secret teaching' often appeared in their allegorisation of the Gospels – their mystical interpretation of the events recorded there. And it was against such allegorisation that Irenaeus wrote most strongly. His main method was to hold fast to the 'canon of truth received at baptism'. This was the 'baptismal creed' – at first, not so much a creed as a series of answers given by the Christian believer, on entering into his new life. What came to be called 'The Apostles' Creed' – the oldest confession of faith – appears to have been formulated around the year 150 AD, and probably originated in Rome. The beliefs stated in it seem to have been carefully defined in order to counteract Gnosticism.

The Gnostics denied a Divine act of Creation. So, in the Creed, there is the statement, "I believe in one God, who *made* heaven and earth." Against the Docetic conception of Christ, is the stated belief, "Christ Jesus, Son of God, was made flesh for our Salvation." To counteract the mystical, subjective tendencies of the Gnostics, there was the affirmation that Christ suffered and was crucified under Pontius Pilate, thus declaring the Saviour to be a person who lived on earth in historical time. And to exclude the belief in the evil of matter, and so in a purely spiritual Resurrection, Catechumens answered that they believed in the Resurrection of the Body, and that Christ would come to judge the living and the dead. It is possible that, had the 'orthodox' Church not felt the need to defend Christian teaching from Gnosticism, the Creed would not have been formulated in that particular way.

Irenaeus summed up his attack on the Gnostics by his affirmation that Scripture – the Scripture then accepted by the Great Church and soon to be almost identical with the present New Testament – together with Apostolic Tradition, constituted the faith by which Christians live.

As can be seen from contemporary and later history, Irenaeus' proofs of a single, guaranteed, unbroken tradition were not irrefutable. But for many they seemed so, and they gave yet greater strength to the ever increasing importance of the central teaching-authority at Rome.

This central authority was forming its Canon of Scripture and beginning to formulate its Creed. Whether these could be understood and acted upon by every type of believer did not present itself as a problem to the first leaders of the Great Church. But it was a problem in the view of some thinkers, and was to appear as a problem running through most of the Christian heresies of the first three centuries.

# VI

## MARCIONITES AND MONTANISTS

Throughout the second century, while some Christian communities were forming themselves into churches and combining to become part of the Great Church, others were following leaders of diverging views and beliefs.

Already in St Paul's time, Christian converts were forming sects, each taking the name of a special teacher: "...everyone of you saith, I am of Paul; and I of Apollos; and I of Cephas; and I of Christ." (1 *Cor* 1, 12). In post-apostolic times the divergences were growing still greater; indeed in some regions it may have been difficult to determine who were the rightful descendants of the first Christian teachers.

One of these divergent groups was that of the Marcionites. Most of what is known about their beliefs comes from the writings of Irenaeus, who attacked them in his book *Adversus Haereses*.

The Marcionites, unlike the Gnostics, formed a Church. This they claimed to be universal, based on the authentic institution of Christ. Marcionite numbers grew rapidly, until in some regions, it seemed that they would outnumber the Great Church. Irenaeus wrote against what appeared to him to be as great a danger to the unity of Christianity as was the teaching of the Valentinian Gnostics. The Marcionites are often depicted as a Gnostic sect, but, though many of their tenets were the same, the kernel of their belief was totally different. The aim of Gnosticism was to teach those, who could be taught, the true knowledge that would restore them to their origin. Christianity was *one* of the ways to do this. The

Marcionites considered themselves to be the only true Christians, and their aim was to preach pure Christianity, which alone could bring salvation. They aimed at a simple, ascetic form of Christianity – a reaction against the speculative and 'mystical' ideas that seemed to them to be spreading everywhere.

Marcion lived between c.130 and 180 AD. The system he taught incorporated some of the Gnostic doctrines which he had studied. He accepted the Gnostic principle of Dualism: Matter was hostile to the Good. This meant that the Creator-God, the 'Demiurge', was limited and evil; and his material creation was therefore evil.

Accordng to Marcion's system, man was the creation of this stern and wrathful God, who gave him a Law which was impossible to keep, so that he lay under a curse. The Higher God of Goodness – the First Principle – took pity on man and sent his Son to rescue him. This manifestation of the Supreme God was clothed in the phantom body of a man of thirty-three years of age, whom the 'Demiurge' caused to be crucified. Following gnostic ideas, this was a Docetic Christ, a purely spiritual being, not subject to the birth and death of an ordinary man. The Risen Christ charged the 'Demiurge' with acting against his own Law. And so, to make amends, the 'Demiurge' had to deliver to the 'Good God' the souls of the redeemed who had died. To draw the living to Himself the 'Good God' raised up Paul, who was the only one who understood the doctrine of the God of Love and the God of Law.

Marcion held that St Paul alone knew and kept the true traditions of Christ. He shared this belief, with many of the Gnostic schools, who regarded St Paul as their founder. St Paul had drawn an antithesis between the servitude of the Law and the freedom of grace, and this was interpreted by Marcion as an antithesis between the justice of the God of the Old Testament, (identified with the 'Demiurge'), and the love of the Good and Supreme God.

At this time the 'Great Church', comprising those churches

which accepted the leadership of Rome and a common Apostolic tradition, was still without a completely fixed canon of
scripture, though it had its collection of Apostolic literature,
which included the letters of St Paul, as well, of course, as the
four Gospels. As had been done from the very first days, the
Christian communities also read extracts from the Law and the
Prophets.

Marcion probably had a fixed canon of scripture. In his
Church, the *Gospel of Truth* was read, St Paul's epistles (exclu-
ding the Pastoral letters), and, of the four Gospels, only an
edited version of St Luke. In I *Corinthians* XI 23-26, St Paul was
shown to have received an account of the Last Supper 'from
the Lord'. The account most similar to this is found in St
Luke's Gospel, which convinced Marcion that that Gospel was
written by St Paul.

The main purpose in the Marcionites' collection of scripture
was to emphasise the love and forgiveness of God which they
considered best reflected in St Luke's Gospel. They held that
the Old Testament scriptures, which were read in the 'Catholic' churches, were opposed to the teaching of mercy, which
was for them the hallmark of true Christianity. Anything
which they found in St Luke's Gospel or in St Paul's letters to
be at variance with their conception of Christian teaching they
attributed to falsifications introduced by Judaisers and by
those Apostles who opposed Paul.

Marcion believed that God had raised him up to preach
again the true Gospel and to bring the Church back to an
understanding of St Paul's teaching. Man must put his trust in
the 'Good God' and renounce the 'Demiurge'. This renunciation of the 'God of Matter' led to rejection of everything
sensual and so to a strict asceticism. The Marcionites, like the
Gnostics, made a division between the 'Perfect' and the other
believers. For them, the 'Perfect' were those who were baptised and who thenceforth had to remain celibate. The ordinary believers could live a normal married life and were only
baptised at the time of their death. This Marcionite doctrine

was to reappear in later mediaeval heresies, where similar distinctions were made between grades of adherents.

It was not only their belief in the hostility of Matter and therefore in the necessary rejection of all sensual indulgence that gave rise to these hierarchies; there was also, as in many heresies, the sense that the demands of Christianity were so enormous that they were far above what the mass of people could attain. The Marcionites used their hierarchical system as a solution to this problem, in the same way as the Gnostics had done.

In seeming contradiction to the strictness of their hierarchical rules, the Marcionite Church insisted that only faith in God's love was needed for salvation, humanity having been freed from the legislation of the Old Testament God. This emphasis on a loving, merciful God, rather than on a God of wrath and justice, was what attracted increasing numbers of converts into their community. Marcionite communities spread rapidly, especially in the Eastern part of the Roman Empire, and there were Marcionite churches there throughout the second century and at the beginning of the third. But by the end of the third century Marcionism had either died out or had been engulfed by other sects.

Though some Marcionite doctrines were to have an influence on Christian teachings of later times, it is primarily the great numbers of the Marcionites and the size of their Church that makes the Marcionite heresy important; indeed, in the second century it might have appeared uncertain which would become the continuing Church of Christianity, the Great Church or the Marcionite.

And yet, looking back through history, the Marcionite system is seen to be full of illogicalities and over-simplifications. Its many illogicalities caused its churches to split into factions. Tertullian, writing a few decades after Irenaeus, said: "Marcionites make churches as wasps make nests" (Tertullian, Adv. Marc.). Proliferation and division may well be the distinguishing marks of what constitutes a heresy.

Another group of Christians who broke away from the main Church in the second half of the second century were the Montanists. This sect was not so much heretical in doctrine as reformist in attitude. Like the Marcionites they sought a return to the purity of original Christianity, declaring that the rules governing the ethical behaviour of Christians were not given through the authority of bishops and Church institutions, but by God alone, speaking through inspired prophets.

Montanus, their founder, who appeared in Phrygia about the year 156 AD, claimed to be in line with the succession of prophets. His declared mission was to bring about a return to the simplicity of the early Church and to announce the fulfilment of the prophecy of Pentecost.

The dispensation of the Holy Spirit was to replace that of Christ. The final outpouring of the Spirit, the Montanists believed, was happening at that very moment in Phrygia. Some even claimed that Montanus was the incarnation of the Spirit; and two of his followers, Prisca and Maximillia, were said to be prophetesses, uttering the commands of the Holy Ghost in 'spiritual' frenzy. All who 'had the Spirit' were called prophets.

During the second century the Great Church was carefully formulating its doctrines and elaborating its institutions of administration. The Montanists reacted against these developments. They aimed at a freer, more emotional form of religion, requiring ecstasy in worship, prophetic visions from their leaders and a 'speaking with tongues' by the 'faithful' – not unlike some of the 'charismatic' groups today.

Although Christianity was still an unauthorised sect in the Roman Empire and subject to periodic persecutions, nevertheless, by this time – the end of the second century – the numbers of Christians were growing dramatically. They were no longer small, closed communities of heroic 'saints', scattered throughout the Empire. Growth in numbers meant dilution, as it always has. The new Christian converts were less strict in their behaviour; they were often involved in worldly occupations; and many bishops wished to make it easier and less demanding to become a Christian.

Montanus sought a higher standard of morality. He wanted to impose stricter rules for fasting and marriage and, for the 'true Christian', entire separation from the world. There were no accepted doctrines that he denied, no scriptures that he repudiated, but he withdrew from what he considered to be a secular Church in order to found his own. At the beginning of the third century, Tertullian, the great jurist-historian and former writer against heresies, joined the Montanists. He looked for a Church of exceptional and demanding moral standards.

The underlying question seemed to be – should the Church be a society of separated religious devotees or should its members be free to follow worldly occupations? The Montanists saw the Christian Church as the former, but the Great Church, as a whole, decided for the latter. Baptised Christians were entering into ordinary Roman life; and the Church was taking Roman organisation, philosophy and jurisprudence into its service.

By the end of the century the Montanist Church appeared as an even more powerful rival to the Catholic Church than the Marcionites had been. Many Christians were now asking themselves whether the Montanists or the Catholics were the true heirs of Christ.

Fifty years previously, when Montanus lived, there was as yet no organisation which could claim general acceptance as the Catholic Church, divinely instituted; and no fixed canon of New Testament Scripture. Christianity was still in a fluid state. Irenaeus' great work against heresies had not yet been written. There appeared then to be merely disagreement between those holding different interpretations and beliefs, rather than a clear line between 'orthodox' and 'heretic'. So that, in Montanus' time, it was not difficult for separated groups of Christians to live in accordance with their own particular views of strict Christian behaviour, and worship as they thought fit.

By the turn of the century however, the Great Church was already an institution for administration and for teaching. Some writings were considered canonical and some were not. The beliefs and practices of the Montanists were then held to be heretical, their 'prophets' and prophecies condemned, and the sect itself excommunicated, although small Montanist communities survived in Phrygia until the fourth century.

Though an institutional Church with a formulated body of dogmatic teaching was precisely what the Montanists were opposing, it was their own existence and actions that helped to create it. As was the case with other great heresies, in trying to combat them Church leaders were forced to articulate their beliefs in clear-cut doctrines. And to end the danger of divisions which could destroy a unified Church these doctrines were issued in the form of dogma, that is to say, as doctrines, the belief in which is binding.

By the time the third century opened, there was already an established collection of 'orthodox' beliefs, binding on those who considered themselves part of the Catholic Church; 'catholic' was now synonymous with 'orthodox' Christianity. The Apostles' Creed had been formulated, and adherence to it was obligatory.

So now our questions emerge in greater clarity. In view of all that took place in the first two centuries, how much was the establishment of doctrine and institution merely the result of reaction to circumstance and to the words and deeds of others? Was it a necessary development inherent in the very religion itself? If it was, did this development lead to new insights and understanding, and so to true growth? Or did strict formulation lead to distortion? Was St Hilary, Gallic bishop of the fourth century, right when he said, "The error of others compels *us* to err in daring to embody, in human terms, truths which ought to be hidden in the silent veneration of the heart." (Hilary, *De Trinitate* 2.ii.7). Even granting some inevitable distortion, was this a necessary price to pay for the continuation of a world-religion, which would otherwise have evaporated into a collection of divergent sects? Was logical definition essential to an institutional Church, which alone could give the Christian religion continuity?

The Montanists were reacting against the increasing legalism and intellectualism of the Great Church. An institutional Church, inheriting much that was practically useful from the law and administration of the Roman Empire, was, in their eyes, something wholly different from the early Church, established by Christ. So who was following the mainstream?

Were the Montanists right in thinking that the Christian Church should be a small body of completely dedicated Christians, rather than a vast collection of people of all types and standards? Quality, not quantity, was what they aimed at. If the Montanists had become the most powerful force among second-century Christians, the history of the Christian Church might have been very different. A Montanist Church, if remaining true to its tenets, would not have become a temporal power – there would have been little connection with Emperors and Kings. But would a Montanist Church, driving out the mediocre and the worldly, have survived through eighteen centuries?

# VII

# MANICHAEISM

At the beginning of the third century the church at Rome was generally regarded as the centre from whence accepted interpretations of doctrine and forms of teaching should be given to the daughter-churches. This was how Irenaeus had envisaged it. But it was not until the express formulation of Pope Leo I in the fifth century that the Pope's authority was said to rest on the papal succession from St Peter. Irenaeus had already stressed the importance of this doctrine, but it had not yet been authoritatively stated.

In the centuries before Leo there were many controversies concerning Christian theology and these had their effect on subsequent Church history. They were also interwoven with the establishment of Christianity as the Empire's official religion. But, before turning to the theological controversies, which were already beginning even in the second century, and to the great historic change which was to take place in the fortunes of the Christian Church, there is another 'heretical' system that must be considered. This system is important because it is closely connected with Gnosticism, with 'hierarchies', and with the way in which 'searchers after truth' thought they should or should not live. This religious system is Manichaeism.

Manichaeism is not a 'heresy' in the strict meaning of the term, since the Manichees did not consider themselves to be Christians; but in a sense, they were part of the Church. Theirs was a type of secret society. Their aim was to find the inner connection between all religions, so they were allowed, by their own rules, to adopt the language of the religion prevailing where they lived and outwardly to conform to it.

It is said that Mani, the founder, professed to have blended Christian teachings with those of the Persian Magi. His was to be the new and perfect religion. Yet even considered as a separate religion, Manichaeism must be included here, because of its connection with and influence on Christian doctrines, both 'orthodox' and 'heretical', and because of the effect it had on Christians contemporary with it and on their descendants of later ages.

Mani was born in Persia about 215 A D, and was said to come from a well-to-do Persian family. About the year 280, he moved into the eastern provinces of the Graeco-Roman Empire to teach and spread his religious ideas. He had studied Persian Magism, had been to India and had heard a little about Buddhism. It seems that he had learned about Christianity from Basilidean Gnostic sects and through the Marcionite Churches. Most of what is known about Manichaeism comes from fourth-century Roman documents and from Moslem historians of the tenth century. There were many Manichaean writings known to the Moslems which are now lost; many were destroyed by the Christian bishops.

Mani's system and mythology were based on a dualistic conception of the Universe in accordance with the Zoroastrian teaching of the Persian Magi. The world is clearly full of terrifying contradictions, and, for the Manichees, the only possible explanation for this lies in the existence of two separate cosmic kingdoms – the one of Light, the other of Darkness. In the Manichaean system, the physical and the ethical are not distinguished one from the other. Light and Goodness are the same, as are Evil and Darkness. There are two Rulers in the Universe. The Kingdom of Light is ruled by the good Primal God. The Kingdom of Darkness is another spiritual Kingdom, and Satan and the demons are born from it. The two Kingdoms are opposed for all eternity.

According to the Manichaean myth, Satan invaded the Kingdom of Light. To fight against him, God created Primal

Man, who was, for the Manichees, an Archetype – an original ideal pattern, not the first human being. Satan overcame his opponent and, although Primal Man was rescued by God, Satan robbed him of some particles of light and mingled these with five elements of the dark world. Out of these mixed elements God formed the visible world in order to deliver the imprisoned light. Primal Man and his helping spirits dwell in the Sun, and the twelve constellations collect any particles of light set free and pour them into the Sun. Here they are purified and can attain to God.

The first man of human kind, Adam, was engendered by Satan in conjuction with 'sin'. But Satan drove into him the particles of stolen light so as to be able to dominate these sparks more securely. Eve was created to be Adam's companion; she also had a spark of light within her, although a smaller one. The heavenly spirits took the human beings under their care and sent aeons (spiritual powers) to help them. These took the visible forms of prophets. As in the Gnostic systems, their purpose in coming was to instruct humanity as to its true nature.

In the Manichaean system, these prophets were sometimes named Adam, Noah, Abraham, Zoroaster, Buddha, Jesus, Paul. Mani was the last and the greatest. They could only save Man and set free the Light within by imparting true gnosis of his nature and his forces. The light set free would ascend to God. If man is not redeemed in his life-time, then he must go through further cycles of life after death to purify himself. When all light is united with God, the angels will withdraw from the world; a huge conflagration will destroy the material Universe, and again there will be, as at first, complete separation of the two Spiritual Kingdoms.

The Manichaean conception of Christianity seems to have been influenced by Marcionite teaching, in its antagonism to the Old Testament and to the 'Old Testament God'. The Docetic Christ of the Manichees is similar to the Marcionite – "a divine being clothed in the semblance of Man". This Docetism also connects the Manichees with Gnosticism; and the kernel of the Manichaean belief is close to the gnostic tenet that there is within mankind that which must be freed in order to return to its Giver. But in the Manichaean system, it was only through Mani, who was continuing the work of the helpers from Heaven, that the separation of Light from Darkness could be completed – only through him and his imitators, 'the elect'.

Again, as in the Gnostic systems, there were different grades among believers. All were not of the same stature, nor had they the same obligations imposed upon them. In the Manichaean system, the emphasis seems to have been on what was required of the higher grades, but no one was in the category of the hopeless. The lowest grades had a hope of reincarnation, and, in a new cycle of life, could look for liberation.

There were five grades of Manichees. The first three included the teachers, or 'Sons of Meekness'. They were called the *Perfecti,* or the *Electi.* Then came the Administrators, the 'Sons of Knowledge or Discernment' enlightened by the Sun, who were the bishops and priests. The last grade consisted of the Elders, the 'Sons of Understanding or Intelligence', who were the presbyters. The Administrators and the Elders together were called the *Auditori* – the Hearers. The teachers or 'Sons of Meekness' were Mani himself and his successors.

The dualism of the Manichees and their belief in Matter as the prison of light gave rise to a strict asceticism in their rules of conduct. They could not eat flesh, and marriage and procreation were condemned, since with the engendering of souls yet more particles of light would be imprisoned.

But it was only the Electi who obeyed these and other obligations and it was only they who could be called Manichees in the strict sense. The *Auditori* had fewer demands made upon them. They were enjoined to abstain from lying, adultery, murder, doubt and slackness, and to keep a certain number of fasts. Otherwise they could live an easier life. The *Auditori* had to treat the *Perfecti* with the greatest respect, almost amounting to worship, for the *Perfecti* were redeemers. Only they had full knowledge of religious truths and alone could intercede for others.

Manichaeism spread rapidly throughout the Roman Empire and far into Asia. By the beginning of the fourth century, the large number of its members made it appear as one of the great religions claiming adherence. There was a single head over the five grades of believers – the Manichaean Pope; and for many centuries there was a Manichaean Pope in Babylon.

The Marcionites were numerous among the converts to Manichaeism; for much of its teaching was akin to their own and was probably originally taken from it. By the end of the third century most of the surviving Marcionite churches were incorporated into the Manichaean community.

Manichaeism won especially large numbers of followers from the cultured and intellectual circles in the Graeco-Roman Empire. It seemed to provide an intelligent philosophy and a repudiation of the anthropomorphism of the Old Testament Scriptures. In Rome and in North Africa, many people, especially among the scholars and teachers, turned to Manichaeism. The most famous convert was St Augustine, who, for nine years, was one of the *Auditori*.

St Augustine had been taught about Christianity as a child, but had never become a Christian, nor pursued Christian ideas as a young man and a student. When he first met the Manichaean system he felt that these ideas gave him an explanation of the meaning of the world and of the purpose of his existence. But later he became dissatisfied with the explanations given in the Manichaean cosmic myth. It seemed to him that the conception of rival worlds of Light and Darkness and of the war between them only pushed the question of Good and Evil one stage further back and answered nothing. He could not see how an all-perfect God could be attacked and invaded by a Spirit of Darkness.

When St Augustine became a Christian his devotion to, and subsequent rejection of Manichaeism had some influence on the way he expounded Christian doctrine. Fundamental to his teaching was the universal, all-embracing power of God the Creator, and the powerlessness and sinfulness of human beings whose evil lay within, not in the world without; men and women could not blame an external power for their own errors and wrongdoing.

The invasion of North Africa by the Vandals in the fifth century saw the end of Manichaeism there, but Manichaean communities continued to exist in the Byzantine Empire in the East, and many settled in Bulgaria and Armenia. It is probable that the fifth century Paulicians and Bogomils of those regions, who were thought of as heretical Christians, were these same Manichaean sects under other names. They too had their *Perfecti* and their *Auditori*, they believed in a Docetic Christ and in the evil of Matter. The eleventh-century Crusaders found Paulician sects in Syria and Palestine, and there were still Bogomils in Russia in the nineteenth century.

The Byzantine Emperors issued edicts condemning Manichees to death. From the end of the fifth century Manichaeism could be said to have 'gone underground' until it reappeared among the Cathars in southern France and Spain in the eleventh century. This resurgence was probably encouraged by the Paulicians and Bogomils of the East, whose ideas were brought into the West along the East-West trade routes. The Church theologians of that time described all such heretics as Manichees.

The Cathars had the same affinity with Gnostic Christianity as had the Manichees, and much of their philosophy and doctrine was Manichaean. Men were created as a result of a war in heaven, for Satan – or sometimes the evil God of the Old Testament – had imprisoned heavenly spirits in terrestrial bodies. The Cathars certainly considered themselves Christians, but they believed in two Eternal Powers – the Good God and the Evil Creator or the Prince of Darkness. Matter was held to be hostile to the Good, and this conception, of the eternal antagonism between Matter and Spirit, resulted in

belief in a Docetic Christ; for a Holy Christ could not assume
flesh. Hostility to Matter, and therefore to the flesh, led to an
imposition of rules of strict ascetism, too difficult for the
ordinary believer to follow. The Cathars, therefore, accepted a
hierarchy of believers in similar fashion to the Manichees.

This hierarchy of believers was extremely important in
Catharism. The system was based on the distinction between a
pure élite (the *perfecti* or *boni homines*) and the ordinary mass of
believers (the *credenti*). The *perfecti* were initiated by receiving
the sacrament called the *consolamentum,* (the consolation),
which the Cathars referred to as 'heretication'. Once hereti-
cated the *bonhomme* had to accept many disciplines – an austere
manner of living, strict dietary rules and permanent celibacy –
so that only those seriously seeking perfection would receive
the *consolamentum* while still in active life. The ordinary *cre-
dentes* received it only when death was near. The *perfecti* had the
power to give blessings and to intercede for the believers, and
were venerated and even worshipped by them.

The Cathars' dualism led them to believe that material
objects could have no connection with Spirit. So they totally
rejected all Catholic sacraments and aids to worship. The use
of water in baptism they thought to be wrong. Their *consolamentum* was given through "a book and through words", that
is, by the laying on of hands, and by the placing of the Gospel
on the head. The Cross was on no account to be venerated, as it
was made of wood, and, in any case, Christ had not suffered
upon it. The use of bread and wine in the Eucharist was
condemned by them.

The Cathars, like the Gnostics, concentrated on the use of
allegory within Christian doctrine. For them there was no
resurrection of the flesh. They held that true resurrection lay in
the spiritual baptism bequeathed by Christ to the *boni homines.*
Death brought no liberation, unless man became a new crea-
ture – a vehicle of the Paraclete, the Holy Spirit – in the same
way as Christ. This world was the only true Purgatory and
Hell, as it was the antithesis of the eternal world of Christ's

Peace. Also, for the Cathars as for the Manichees the Crucifixion was symbolic, because the account of the suffering of
Jesus was held to be the symbolic account of the universal soul
diffused through nature and suffering from its association with
Matter.

The whole movement was directed against the Catholic
Church, because the Cathars, or Albigensians as they were
also called, believed that the Great Church had departed from
the original true teaching about Christ and his revelation and
had become immersed in materialism. They held the sacer-
dotal system – the institution of the priesthood – to be wicked
and wrong, because only the *boni homines,* the 'Good Men',
could lead believers through purification to salvation.

Measures taken to combat the Cathar, or Albigensian,
heresy had their repercussions in Church history. The need to
compete with the powerful influence of the Cathar *boni
homines* was probably a factor in making absolute the Rule of
Celibacy for the clergy. But it was the action which the
Church took to stamp out these heresies that had the most
far-reaching effects. This action included the establishment of
the Inquisition. The crime of high treason against God was
now specifically equated with high treason against the State,
and this was to be the law in Europe for many centuries. Both
crimes were punishable by death and, in both cases, torture
was held to be allowable for the extortion of confessions. The
Pope, in the third Lateran Council, also proclaimed a Crusade
against the Albigensian heretics. The King of France and the
French nobles of the North seized this opportunity to show
their loyalty to the Church and, at the same time, to carry out
their policy of subduing the South, the land of the heretics.
This they did with extraordinary cruelty.

The Cathar sects existed much later than the fifth century,
but they are clearly descended from the Manichees and,
through them, from the Gnostics and Marcionites, whose
ideas were thus carried on through the ages. Even the Knights
Templar in the fourteenth century were accused of Mani-

chaeism. Therefore, although outside the period of this book, the Cathar heresy is included in it because of two important groups of queries to which it gives rise.

With the suppression of the Albigensians and Cathars in the fourteenth century, Manichaeism, as a religion or begetter of heretical sects, finally vanished, but its major tenet has not. There remains the perennial problem of Good and Evil in the Universe. The simplistic Manichaean solution – the opposing Kingdoms of Light and Darkness – is still the belief of many, although they may not, perhaps, consciously realise it. It is certainly not 'orthodox' Christian doctrine. But the status and dominion of the Prince of Darkness has never been satisfactorily defined. Has the Church ever completely erased the influence of the Manichees?

The suppression of the Albigensians and Cathars, and the Inquisition that developed out of that suppression, are examples of the distortions which Christianity – called the 'Religion of Resplendent Love' – has suffered throughout its history. And so the second group of queries cannot be avoided. How was it possible for the Church to live through such an episode and maintain such an institution and yet for Christianity still to survive? Could it be that without the suppression of these divisive and anti-sacerdotal sects an institutional Church would have disappeared? But even were that so, did these distortions of the Christian religion mean that its future development might be impaired?

# VIII

## 'OFFICIAL' CHRISTIANITY; AND THE DONATISTS

We must now return to the series of events in the fourth century that changed the course of Christianity's history and, possibly, even its future development; for events, as well as ideas, affected the formation of 'orthodox' doctrine. Christianity was born in an outlying part of the Roman Empire and its institutions and doctrines were being formed at a time of great change within it. The greatest change, of course, and the one which had the most profound effect on 'orthodox' Christianity, was the adoption of the Christian religion as an official – later *the* official – religion of the Empire. From that time on, the relation of the Christian Church to secular rulers, as well as the growth of the Church's own secular power, was bound to influence the development of the Christian religion itself.

The Roman authorities had, from the first, regarded Christianity as a subversive sect, although it was some years before they distinguished Christians from Jews. The Christians, like the Jews, refused to worship the Roman gods or the Emperor, and so they were 'atheists' and 'haters of humanity'. In addition, they appeared to be a secret society – an anathema to the Romans. Simply being a Christian was a crime against the state. Pliny, governor of Bythinia in III to 131 AD, asked the Emperor Trajan if all Christians should be automatically punished. He was told, "Yes, unless they prove their denial of Christianity by sacrificing to the gods – then they can go free."

Large numbers of Christians did not take this easy road. Throughout the next centuries there were brutal persecutions, only intermittently followed by periods of peace; the Diocletian persecutions, at the beginning of the fourth century, being among the most terrible. During this time the measures taken to stamp out Christianity seemed to have had the reverse effect. The number of Christians in the Empire continued to grow, in part due to the wonder and admiration evoked by their amazing courage, and in part to their own determined resistance, aroused by the attacks made upon them. But they were still a barely tolerated minority, often in danger, and always under suspicion. In 313, as a result of an edict from the Emperor at Rome, the position changed completely.

Constantine, the commander of the Western Provinces – Gaul, Spain and Britain – had proved himself victorious in the struggle for power among the Roman generals after the death of Diocletian. His famous march on Rome in 312 gained him mastership of that city and of the whole of the West. The following year, with Licinius, his co-emperor in the East, he issued the Edict of Milan, which proclaimed that "Christians, and all others, should have liberty to follow the mode of religion which to each of them appeared best." Constantine had decided to protect and support the Christians, and therefore they were specifically mentioned in the text of the Edict. All appropriated property was to be restored to them, and they were to receive complete and unconditional toleration. The Christian Church had now become an accepted institution of the Empire.

In his *Ecclesiastical History,* completed in about 325, Eusebius, Bishop of Caesarea, tells of the dream or vision, which decided Constantine to march on Rome. In this vision, Constantine is said to have seen a flaming cross appear in the sky; inscribed upon it were the words, "By this, conquer". According to Eusebius it was this vision, and the success granted by his obedience to it, that led Constantine to support Christianity, and finally, just before his death, to be baptised.

In Constantine's conversion, no one can know how much was due to religious conviction, how much to superstition, how much to political ambition. It seems that the moral strength of the Christians and their higher standards of morality impressed Constantine, so that he was almost certainly sincere in his admiration for Christianity and, indeed, he had his children educated as Christians. He was also aware that, with the crumbling of civic authority throughout the Empire, and with barbarian tribes continually encroaching, the power to whom people turned for their safety and well-being was the Christian Bishop.

From the post-Apostolic age onward the ideal of a hierarchical order under a divine Apostolic authority had been the governing principle in the administration of the Christian churches that owed allegiance to the Great Church at Rome. Through their insistence on social order and discipline, the Christian communities were able to organise themselves in a time of general disintegration. It is probable that Constantine became convinced that hope for the future lay in the determination and orderliness of Christianity and that he wanted to enlist its growing strength in the service of the Empire. His aim in government was to preserve some form of unity, and it may have been partly for such reasons of policy that he accepted the Christian religion. In a letter which he wrote to the provincial governors, he declared that he had been divinely raised up in order to destroy the enemies of Christianity, who would otherwise have ruined the Empire.

Whatever Constantine's motives, in 313, Christians were given freedom to worship as they wished and, after the death of Licinius in 324, when Constantine became sole ruler of East and West, Christianity was made an official religion of the Roman Empire. A year or two later Constantine decided to move the capital of the Empire from Rome to the East, laying the foundations of Constantinople on the site of ancient Byzantium. Constantine may have regarded the city of Rome as a stronghold of paganism; most of the Roman Senate still clung to the old traditions and, if Rome were to remain his capital, a smooth change over to official Christianity, might have been impossible. The new order in the Empire was

inaugurated by the building of a new capital, dedicated to
Christ and the Blessed Virgin.

But the unity that Constantine hoped for did not materialise.
The controversies between different groups of Christians and
between the followers of disputing theologians even caused
division within his Empire. Constantine bent all his energies
towards ending these divisions. In his opinion, the Emperor,
by virtue of his office, had the right to intervene in such
controversies and to preside over the councils convened to
settle them. By presiding over the ecumenical councils of
bishops coming from all parts of the Empire, Constantine
emphasised the fact that he identified himself with Christianity.

Eusebius, who wrote the official Christian panegyric of
Constantine, described him, in his History of the Emperor, as
"God's dearly beloved", and called opposition to him opposition to God's Own. The Emperor, head of State, appeared, in
Eusebius' eyes, as representative of Christianity. Constantine,
himself, wanted to show that, by virtue of his Imperial office,
he was supreme in ecclesiastical affairs, hoping thereby to
mould the Church into an instrument for consolidating the
absolute power of the Emperor. But at this time the main body
of Christian bishops, from the East as well as from the West,
did not consider themselves servants of the Imperial Government.

Constantine was wrong in his assumption that political
compromises, instituted by himself, could solve theological
disputes. Though it was the Emperor who summoned them
and who chose the subjects they were to discuss, the councils
tended to encourage rather than to diminish the independent
attitude of the Christian bishops. These Councils were the first
representative deliberating assemblies that had ever existed. The
Church appeared as the opponent of state absolutism rather
than as its supporter. By the time Christianity became the
official religion of the Empire, the power of the bishops had
become enormous. In his diocese the bishop commanded
almost supernatural prestige; he was the popular choice of

his people and he now had official powers of jurisdiction over his clergy and over any other case brought before him. Because the Church in the fourth century, through this far-reaching power of the bishops, had become an indispensable part of the social welfare of the State, it seemed at times that it would even become an organ of the Imperial Government. This was largely what happened in the eastern part of the Empire, after the fall of Rome; the Byzantine Church and State became bound together. But this did not happen in the West.

The move of the Imperial Capital from Rome to Constantinople increased the tendency of East and West to separate, and, by the fifth century, the Eastern Churches turned towards the Emperor and Patriarch at Constantinople for spiritual leadership, rather than to Rome. But the relationship between the Eastern Orthodox Churches and the Catholic Church of Rome, leading to their eventual schism, belongs to later history, and so will not be entered into here.

The Western Church never became united with the State in the same way as the Byzantine. The departure of the seat of government to Constantinople meant more independence for the head of the Catholic Church in Rome. St Ambrose, Bishop of Milan at the end of the fourth century, one of the great leaders in the Western Church, taught that the law of the Church could only be administered by the bishops and that even the Emperor was subject to their authority. "The Emperor," as he said, "is within the Church, not over it."

Nevertheless, St Ambrose was intensely loyal to the Emperor of his day. His ideal was a Christian state in which a Christian Church was allied to a Christian Imperial Power. But the seed of the future struggle between Church and State, Pope and Emperor, had already been sown by Constantine.

Official recognition of an institutional Church, and official grants of jurisdiction and privilege to it, meant that the Church was bound to connect itself with state institutions. Both co-operation and opposition would affect its nature, whatever its development in the distant future. These effects showed themselves not so much in specific doctrines, as in the general conception of the Church held by Church leaders, themselves, and by the public at large. The Justice of God would tend to be inextricably entwined, in the minds of many, both learned and simple, with the needs of the institution. For others, Holy Church, divinely ordained, had to be kept separate in their thoughts from the Church organisation as they experienced it.

In the first centuries AD, it had been hazardous to be a Christian; embracing Christianity had entailed a life of hardship and danger. After 315, the Christian community became a respectable body within society. This inevitably increased the amount of worldliness in the Church and the number of purely nominal Christians within it. Because of this, some felt that life had become too easy and that they were not following their true Christian path of sacrifice. This reaction against worldliness and ease was the strongest motive force in the fourth-century 'Flight to the Desert', in which hermitages and monasteries were founded in the most inaccessible parts of Egypt. The institution of monasticism, which began in the Egyptian desert, spread rapidly, both in the East and in the West.

The Gnostic and Manichaean doctrine of Pure Spirit escaping from hostile Matter was also an unconscious influence in fourth century asceticism. In this context struggle against the flesh was essential for salvation. After Christianity's official recognition life had become too materialistic, in the eyes of the devout, who felt that the struggle should be carried on through special means. There was also the broader concept that a perfect Christian should be totally dedicated, and withdrawal from the present comfortable world seemed the only way to achieve this.

So the monastic ideal was born. Not everyone could aspire to such an heroic way of life; but, in the fourth century, it was accepted that it was the highest calling. The hermits and the monks were regarded as the model for Christians. There came to be a distinction between the 'religious' and the 'secular' life.

Then "the monk was the superman – the ordinary cleric and layman followed the same ideal at a distance." (Christopher Dawson, *The Making of Europe*).

Worldliness and political entanglement were not the only dangers involved in becoming an official religion of the Empire; there was another yet greater. It was not till the twelfth century that the Church and the secular power combined together to punish what was held to be treason against God and State – that is to say, heresy. But, already in the fourth century, a persecuted Church had turned persecutor. Those who disagreed with 'orthodox' teachings were stripped of their authority and exiled. In one instance, when all persuasion had failed to bring the dissenters back into the fold, Church and State joined to put them down by force.

These dissenters were the Donatists.

The Christian religion, which Constantine had supposed would unify the Empire, was failing to do so. Almost the first act of the Emperor, after he had legalised that religion, was to send an Imperial Commissioner to North Africa, to investigate a dispute which was threatening to cause dangerous division. There were rival bishops with rival churches, and fierce antagonism between their respective followers.

The Donatist controversy was a continuation of a third-century dissension led by one Novatian, a presbyter of the Roman Church. In the persecutions of Decius, in 250, many Christians had apostasised and, when peace was restored, had sought readmission into the Church. Novatian maintained that those who had lapsed could not dispense the Sacraments. The Bishop of Rome disagreed with him and advocated leniency. Novatian set himself up as rival Bishop of Rome and became head of a heretical movement, allying himself with the Montanists.

Fifty years later, in North Africa, a similar conflict arose. In the Diocletian persecutions many had given way and had handed their sacred scriptures over to their persecutors. These were known as *traditori*. One of the *traditori* was consecrated

Bishop of Carthage in 311. A priest, who had withstood the persecutions and remained faithful, was installed as rival bishop by a more rigorous group. His successor, Donatus (from whom 'Donatism' took its name) was charged with ecclesiastical offences at the trial of the rival bishops, which took place in Rome after Constantine's investigation. Donatus was found guilty, and the synod of Arles, presided over by Constantine, confirmed his guilt.

The Imperial Government had proclaimed who was at fault, and the power of the State was now directed against the defeated party. The Donatists were no longer considered merely heretics, but also rebels. Their property was confiscated and they forfeited all civil rights. But they continued to resist and Constantine and his successors were not able to crush them.

A century later St Augustine attempted to reason with the Donatists. He wrote treatises to discuss and refute their ideas and, in 411, arranged a conference at Carthage to resolve their differences. This failed. St Augustine had previously insisted that force should not be used to compel heretics to return to the Church, as the use of force would corrupt the Church itself; the Church would be impregnated with violence. But now he changed his mind. In his view, unity was of overriding importance and had to be maintained or the Church could not function. Without coercion the Donatists would remain cut off and an isolated, hopeless group for ever.

So Church and Government combined to subjugate the rebels, whom persecution made yet more fanatic. A fanatical movement, outlawed by the Imperial Government, inevitably attracted malcontents – fugitive slaves and vagrants – into its ranks. There were outbursts of violence in North Africa, leading almost to civil war. This had to be quelled. For many years the Donatists were coerced and persecuted, but they lingered on and only finally disappeared with the Saracen invasions of North Africa in the seventh century.

Donatism was not only important in its historical implications, but also because of two doctrinal questions inherent in it.

One question brought out by the Donatist struggle concerns the meaning of the Sacraments. Crucial to the Donatist position was the belief that Sacraments administered by the unworthy were invalid. No priest from among the *traditori* could dispense the Eucharist; and baptism or ordination by one of the *traditori* was null and void.

Augustine stated the Catholic Church's position. If the receiver had faith, he would receive a valid Sacrament, even if the priest were unworthy. The Church was merely the custodian of the means of grace. God was the giver, not man. That this was clearly shown by St Augustine to be the Church's view prevented dangers of subjectivity and subjective judgement. The distinction made between the office of priesthood and the person filling that office was, perhaps, one of the factors that enabled the Catholic Church to survive the periods of corruption and political intrigue that have darkened its history.

The other question concerns the meaning of the Church itself. In a sense Donatism was a schism rather than a heresy. The Donatists held to the 'orthodox' teachings of the Great Church. They separated themselves from it on the issue of who was the truly appointed bishop. But their attitude towards this issue emphasised the old point of conflict: was the Church for the perfect, or was it a Church for all levels of men? Should only good people be recognised as members of a divine society?

The Donatists called themselves the 'communion of saints'. The Catholic Church, according to them, was tainted with worldliness and unworthy members destroyed the Church's holiness. The Donatist Church was holy and so it was the one true Church of God. A holy Church could not include unholy members.

St Augustine put forward the opposing view. In his exposition he described how the contradiction could be resolved.

The Donatists, he said, had misunderstood the Church's holiness. It is not perfect here and now, but is a sign of what is to be. It is true that only saints compose the *true* Church, the Body of Christ, as described by St Paul; but in the Church as it exists on earth there are both good and bad – the tares have to grow along with the wheat. The Church alone has power to cleanse, and outside is nothing. But 'inside' and 'outside' is a matter of heart, not words. 'Outside the Church' means outside the 'elect' – but the *visible* Church is not the 'elect.' Some may be 'elect' who do not yet appear to be, and some may seem 'elect' who are not. The Church was in all the world, not in one corner of Africa. The 'elect' who *are* the Holy Church, cannot be the subject of human judgement. People must accept the Church on earth; God alone can judge the 'elect'.

So St Augustine answered the Donatists. By the end of the fifth century their numbers had dwindled and they gradually faded out of history. But though their ultra-strict standards and lack of leniency turned them into a narrow and fanatical sect, their views cannot be completely disregarded. In the very early days of Christianity it was necessary for catechumens to go through a tough and demanding training before they gained the special privilege of being baptised; and the catechumens would make great sacrifices for this privilege. Is it possible that when demands are light and all is made easy what is given is valued less?

Again the problem arises: was there one Christianity for the strenuous seekers after Truth, and another for the mediocre; and was the religion of the worldly a different form of Christianity from that of the dedicated?

The conception of monasticism was not given by the Church as an answer to these particular questions. The difference between the life of the 'religious' and the secular life was not part of Church doctrine. The institution of monasticism grew out of a general reaction among Christians to the worldliness of Christianity as a state religion.

But were the high demands of such a high religion only to be met by the few, while less was demanded from the majority of weak and cowardly believers? The Donatists, like the Montanists, would not allow that believers of this sort could be part of a Christian community at all. In the view of these sects, spiritual quality was being sacrificed by the Great Church for the sake of unity and universality; in their view also, the worldliness and political entanglement, which resulted from the Church's connection with the imperial government, was too great a price to pay for the Church's continuity. These were contentions that would appear throughout the Church's history.

# IX

# THE NATURE OF GOD
# – ARIANISM

Constantine's Edict of Toleration of 311 A D brought physical peace to the Christians in the Empire. But this very security and absence of danger allowed room for internal controversy. The fourth century was a time of fierce theological debate.

The Catholic Church, in the sense of a 'universal' Church based on Apostolic tradition, was beginning to be an organised institution, with its own canon of Scripture and body of stated doctrine. Religious disputes were now centred on the formulation of these doctrines though, of course, difference in formulation inevitably leads to difference in belief. Nevertheless, the divergences which were to become heresies were of a different kind from those of earlier centuries.

Heresies are likely to arise when questions are posed which seem to lie beyond the logic of the human mind. The early heresies grew up around the perennial problem of Good and Evil – how to understand it, and how to interpret Christian teaching to explain it. The fourth-century heresies arose out of another seemingly unanswerable problem, though this time a doctrinal one – the meaning of the Trinity and of the Nature of Christ.

The idea of what constituted heresy had changed. Up to the fourth century, the 'orthodox Church' – the 'Great Church' – concentrated on the task of preserving the unity and continuity of Christian teaching. It attacked what it thought to be 'heresy', because that 'heresy' could divide and weaken Christian continuity. Now, a 'heresy' was coming to mean 'a direct denial of what is true'. "We are guarding the Tradition from misinterpretation" has a different emphasis from, "This is the exposition of the Truth, and you are denying it."

But as early as the second century, there began to be questioning about the nature of God, as revealed in the teachings of the New Testament, and these speculations and arguments continued through the succeeding centuries. Yet, though there were different schools of thought about these questions with different names attached to them, at first none of these teachings was considered to be uniquely 'orthodox' and therefore none could be labelled 'heretical'.

The ritual words (taken from *Mat,* xxviii 19), "In the Name of the Father and of the Son and of the Holy Ghost", were used at baptism from the earliest times. Justin Martyr, writing at the beginning of the second century, describes new converts as "receiving the washing with water in the name of God the Father and Lord of the Universe, and of our Lord Jesus Christ and of the Holy Spirit". These words needed explanation.

The practice of worshipping Jesus as Son of God was gradually becoming the accepted form of devotion at Christian gatherings. Theologians had to explain what this meant to pagan enquirers, otherwise Christianity would appear to them to be a return to polytheism. For the Judaeo-Christians, who had been taught from childhood that they were the upholders of monotheism among the pagan nations around them, explanation was also required. A Divine Christ had to be reconciled with the Unity of God. Conflicting explanations were multiplying from the second century onwards, and they form the background to the great controversies of the fourth.

It was the desire to stress the Unity of God and to prevent any development which might lead to abandoning monotheism that motivated a school of thought known as Monarchism. This term was first used by Tertullian, the Christian writer who lived at the end of the second century. He termed 'Monarchists' those to whom the idea of the single rule of God was of such importance that all explanations of the nature of Christ had to be given in this light.

To keep to the strict idea of the Unity of God, the Monarchists accepted either what were called 'Adoptionist' views of Christ or what were called 'Pneumatic'. A division had arisen between those who held that Christ was a man in whom the Spirit of God dwelt, and those who believed that a Divine Spirit assumed human flesh. The Adoptionists accepted the first and held that Christ was a human being, even if miraculously conceived, who was filled with divine power to an intense degree. The man, Jesus, was so completely obedient to this power that he was elevated to the position of Son of God. The Adoptionist Monarchists maintained that with this conception of Christ, there was no difficulty in understanding the Oneness of God the Father.

The other, the Pneumatic school of thought, held that Christ on Earth was the temporary manifestation in human form, of a Divine Redeemer. But the Monarchists, in order to ensure strict adherence to monotheism, adopted what came to be called the Modalist view of God, which in the Eastern Churches was later termed Sabellianism after its protagonist, Sabellius. In this conception, 'the Father' and 'the Son' were held to be different designations of the same subject – that is to say, different aspects or modes of the One God. Before the creation of the world, God should be thought of in His aspect of 'Father' and in connection with His appearance in the world as 'Son'. In his attack on the Modalist Monarchists, Tertullian argued that the logical outcome of their views was that God the Father, Himself, suffered and died on the Cross: and this earned the Modalists the nickname of 'Patripassionists'. Although there was ridicule involved in this attack, Church leaders feared a real danger from the Modalists. If the Divine Substance was so exclusively stressed, the Son and Saviour would have no substance in himself. His humanity would disappear. By the end of the third century Sabellius and his Monarchist followers were regarded as heterodox. Sabellius was condemned, but Sabellianism, in various forms, pervaded the theological disputes of the next century and increased their complications.

Problems were bound to grow as Church writers continued to seek adequate philosophical terminology for their expositions. But all this time Christians were meeting for prayer and worship; instruction was being given; attempts were being made to live life according to Christian precepts. While Church leaders and theologians were trying to find the right formulations, Christian belief and forms of liturgy were taking permanent shape in the churches; for by the second century, Christ, as the Redeemer of mankind, was being worshipped at regular Christian gatherings and petitions of prayer were being addressed to him.

For some Monarchists of the Adoptionist school this seemed a dangerous anti-monotheistic tendency. Paul of Samosata, Patriarch of Antioch at the end of the third century, would not allow prayer to Jesus Christ in his church, nor hymns in Christ's honour. God alone should be worshipped; prayers were to be *through* Christ, as intermediary, between God and man.

But Paul of Samosata came into conflict with the Pope, was condemned and exiled. In this conflict about the nature of Christ, the word *homoousios* (of like substance) – a word that was to assume great importance in the fourth century disputes – was used for the first time. On this occasion, the term was rejected.

The teaching and writings of Origen, the young head of the Alexandrian catechetical school, had been a dominant influence on Christian thinkers at the end of the second and the beginning of the third centuries. Those who, like Paul of Samosata, were stressing above all the humanity of Christ, attacked Origen's teaching for emphasising his Divinity although, strangely enough, Origen's teaching was later to be attacked and condemned by churchmen, who were maintaining that Christ was coequal with God, and who considered that Origen made the Son subordinate.

Origen explained the three Persons as being within the Godhead – the Father, the Unbegotten; the Son, the Wisdom and Power of God, directing the universe; and the Holy Spirit, brought into being by the Father through Christ.

The second-century Gnostics had raised in an acute form the question of the human and divine in Christ. In their schools Christ was a purely Divine Spirit, part of the hierarchy of heavenly beings, whose connection with earth could be understood only in terms of a cosmic myth. Origen, though in sympathy with much Gnostic teaching, wrote to counteract these particular ideas, which he considered a danger to authentic Christian tradition. So in his explanation of the nature of Christ and of Christ's relation to God, Origen was not concerned, as were the Monarchists, in upholding the concept of monotheism, but in giving the true meaning of human salvation.

Central to Origen's teaching was the thesis that "the whole man would not have been saved unless Christ had taken upon himself the whole man." This became an argument of vital importance in the later debates. Although, like the Gnostics, Origen believed in a Divine Christ, Son of God, descended from Heaven, he also held that Christ must have had the soul, the mind and the body of a man. The essence of Christianity for Origen was that Christ "made his humanity divine as a first fruit of the hope that is ours." (Origen, *On the Fundamental Doctrines*).

But profound as Origen's teaching was, it still appeared to leave unanswered the questions of how, in Christ, there existed both the Divine and the human, and what was the relation of Jesus Christ to the One omnipotent God.

Origen accepted that the Logos – the Son, as described in St John's Gospel – was mediator between God and Man and so, in a sense, subordinate to God, the Father of All; and that the Son, the directing power of God, was generated from the Essence of God. This 'subordinationism' was one of the so-called 'heresies' that caused Origen's writings to be condemned in the fifth century.

The relationship between Christ and God, and between

Christ and man, formed the substance of the fourth and fifth-century controversies and, out of these, the heresies of this period.

In studying these controversies and the Councils that attempted to settle them, it often seems that their endless dissensions, condemnations and counter-condemnations were merely theologians' quarrels about the detailed use of words and about minute differences in the 'expression of the inexpressible'.

St Hilary of Poitiers, writing to the Emperor Constantine complained that "Every year, nay every moon, we make new creeds to describe invisible Mysteries. We repent of what we have done, we defend those who repent, we anathematise those whom we defended. We condemn either the doctrine of others in ourselves or our own in that of others; and, reciprocally tearing one another to pieces, we have been the cause of each other's ruin." (Hilarius and Constantium, ı ii c 4, 5, quoted in Gibbon's *Decline and Fall of the Roman Empire* Vol ıı). Attempts to make concise logical statements about 'invisible Mysteries' inevitably lead to logical difficulties. Every formulation brings its own contradiction, or else says virtually nothing.

The teachings in the Gospels told men what they should do in order that the Kingdom of Heaven might come; they did not explain a religious philosophy, nor work out a theory of the Universe. Since human beings have always asked questions, those who accepted and taught the new religion were bound to try to fit their belief and their obedience into a cosmological form, understandable to themselves and to their hearers. Deductions continued to be made from the original teaching given. It was inevitable that the disputes which arose out of this struggle to form a system should be destructive of Christian unity. But minds were made for enquiry and enquiring minds cannot be held back from trying to understand.

In the fourth century the eastern part of the Roman Empire was the main centre of theological discussion. The Greeks, who adopted the new religion, brought with them their love of disputation and logical definition.

Byzantine culture was essentially a religious one and, to the fourth-century Byzantine, the 'heavenly world' and his hopes and fears concerning it, were of far greater importance to him than the political and economic affairs of his city. This explains why the theological controversies of the time were followed with such passionate interest, not only by churchmen but also by the ordinary citizens. The rulers of Heaven obviously commanded greater power than the rulers of earth; and it seemed natural that one should be more concerned about the conditions of eternal life than about the conditions of this one, short and uncertain as it was. "No less an authority than St Gregory Nazianzen has described how, if you went into a shop in Constantinople to buy a loaf, 'the baker, instead of telling you the price, will argue that the Father is greater than the Son. The money-changer will talk about the Begotten and the Unbegotten, instead of giving you your money; and, if you want a bath, the bath-keeper assures you that the Son surely proceeds from nothing.'" (C. Dawson, *The Making of Europe*)

Religious problems occupied so much of daily life that the conception of a separation between Church and State was not possible in the general thinking of the age. Belief in the sacred character of the Emperor had continued from pre-Christian times into the Christian era; and the Emperor saw himself as a Divine Regent: "He felt called upon to guide the human race towards the true religion that he proclaimed and taught." (J. Daniélou, *The First Six Hundred Years*). So the institution by the Emperor of ecumenical councils was considered to be the act not of a political leader, but of the leader of the Christian people. The Emperor was automatically asked to intervene in theological arguments. The general councils were summoned and guided by imperial authority.

Not all bishops, however, were subservient to the Emperor. In the theological controversies of the fourth century there was no straightforward division between churchmen and statesmen; there was a schism of conscience and of divided loyalties.

Arguments about the Trinity and about the relation of

Christ to the Father had been growing in intensity during the opening year of the century. Attempts to explain Christ's divinity were, some thought, leading to the danger that his humanity would be forgotten: Christ would be treated merely as an aspect of God. It was fear of this that led Arius, a priest of Alexandria at the beginning of the fourth century, to protest against what he considered to be the Sabellianism of his Bishop, Alexander, who had said that "God is always; the Son is always; and the Son was present in the Father without birth." One of Arius' aims was to establish the unity and simplicity of God who, as pure Spirit, could have no direct contact with the material world. Therefore, according to Arius, an intermediary was necessary. This was the Son, a created being, though formed before time began. Christ was Divine only by participation in the Divinity of the Father, who was transcendent and above all things. Whereas Origen explained the Divinity of the Son as being within the Godhead, Arius saw Him as an intermediary – a being separate from the Father.

The Bishop of Alexandria called for Arius' excommunication and for the anathematising of his writings. Arius collected around him supporters of his teaching, and rival groups began to form. So began the disputes that led to the great breakaway movement, termed the Arian Heresy, which was to divide the Christian Church and which did not finally disappear until the eighth century.

The Emperor Constantine was alarmed at this further disunity in his Empire; for disunity was what he especially wanted to avoid. He tried to bring the parties together, saying that they were both equally right; but the controversy continued. In 325 Constantine summoned a great council – the first world (ecumenical) council – that of Nicaea. One hundred bishops came from Asia Minor, seventy from Syria and Phoenicia, twenty from Palestine and Egypt, only a few from the Latin West, and two priest-delegates from Rome.

By the close of the council the formula of the creed used for preparing catechumens for baptism in Caesarea had been accepted as the basis for agreement, and the word *homoousios* – of one substance – was adopted to describe the being of Christ. That is to say, Christ was affirmed to be consubstantial with the Father. This – the question of consubstantiality – became the centre of the ensuing controversy; for the Nicene Council had settled nothing. It was on this point that those who accepted the Nicene formula opposed those who supported or tended towards the Arian position.

Arius was excommunicated and sent into exile. But many, who were hostile to the Arian view, were not happy with the adoption of the word *homoousios,* which was not a scriptural term, nor found anywhere in either the Old or the New Testament. The use of this word is the first example of a purely theological definition being set forth as an article for belief. It was the beginning of the trend towards definition of dogmas – for example, the Immaculate Conception – which were not based on scriptural writings but arose from deduction and elucidation, (cf J. Daniélou, *The First Six Hundred Years*).

Immediately after the Council dispersed the Emperor Constantine gave his support to anti-Arian decrees, but still the squabbles continued. The Latin West (including Egypt) accepted peacefully the Nicene definition; but the Greek East was divided into many schools of thought and was harassed by fears of Sabellianism.

Doctrinal and personal quarrels multiplied and the Emperor intervened either to support or to exile the leaders of the conflicting parties. Three years after accepting the decrees of the Council of Nicaea Constantine changed his mind, recalled Arius from exile and supported the anti-Nicene party until the end of his reign.

Succeeding Emperors had varying views, and their varying views affected the life of the Church. Most of them were Arian or else semi-Arian, that is to say, they adopted the formula that the 'Son was *like* unto the Father', 'of like substance but not of the same'. (The word used was *homoiousius* – hence the accusation that the Church was torn apart over a diphthong!) The Emperor Constantius was one of these semi-Arians, and in 360 proclaimed their definition as the official faith of the Empire.

The major opponent of Arianism of all kinds was Athanasius. He came to the Council of Nicaea as a young priest and was consecrated Bishop of Alexandria in 328. Throughout the succeeding stormy years Athanasius was exiled and reinstated many times, and died before Nicene orthodoxy was finally established. But it was his writings that made explicit the root of the conflict and made clear why it was important. The Creed that was ultimately adopted has been named the 'Nicene' or 'Athanasian' Creed.

Athanasius was the protaganist of consubstantiality. He maintained that the Word became man, not that it came *into* a man; because, he said, that if Christ existed in the latter sense, as Arius held, then he was no different from the prophets and saints of old, even if of a higher degree. For Athanasius, Christ must be unique and different in kind from ordinary humanity, even where that humanity had been given Divine grace. The change in the innermost being of man, necessary to restore his lost immortality, could only be effected by God Himself. Escape from final death could only be realised by one who partook of the nature of God. That, Athanasius said, was the purpose of the Incarnation. Therefore, the Son must be of one substance with the Father.

Arius was insistent on affirming the unity and changelessness of God and the necessity never to forget the humanity of Christ and his capacity for change and suffering. There seemed here to be two irreconcilable statements. Only God could redeem and God was changeless; yet Christ, the redeeming intermediary, suffered and died.

In the early stages of the controversy Athanasius maintained that some ideas are beyond our comprehension. "In every step of the enquiry, we are compelled to feel and acknowledge the immeasurable disproportion between the size of the object and the capacity of the human mind." But as the controversies developed he was forced to find definitions for these 'immeasurable ideas'.

As Athanasius saw it, Arius' error was to make the Trinitarian distinctions *outside* the Deity – that is to say, he postulated one Supreme Being and the Son and the Holy Spirit as two lesser beings. Athanasius, like Origen before him, understood the Trinity as differentiation within the Godhead, and accused Arius of portraying a Christ who was neither God nor man, but a superhuman myth figure, thus destroying the Christian scheme of salvation.

Athanasius held that the meaning of the Christian revelation depended on Christ being fully human *and* fully divine. Christ had to be fully human or the whole man could not be saved. "What Christ has not assumed, he has not healed," said St Gregory Nazianzus. He had to be fully divine or there would be no escape from the determinism of nature. The essence of Athanasius' Christianity was expressed in his famous words, "God became man in order that man might become God."

The attraction of Arianism, however, was its apparent simplicity, or rather the impression that it was more rational and easier to comprehend than the opposing system. The use of the word 'Son', had always caused people, almost unconsciously, to envisage a demigod, sent down by the 'Father' and subordinate to Him, so that Arianism seemed to be the form of Christianity that was most naturally understandable. The Nicene doctrines, as expounded by Athanasius, appeared to many to be metaphysical theories, not based on human spiritual experience. Indeed, to some, they seemed to contradict the Old Testament conception of a single 'personal' God.

In the 370s, Basil, Bishop of Caesarea, Gregory of Nyssa, and Gregory Nazianzus, known as 'the three great Cappadocians', were instrumental in bringing the disputing parties together. They reached a formula on which most could agree: 'there was one substance in the Godhead – one ousia; there were three persons – hypostases – not three gods, but one, to be found equally and identically in the Father, Son and Holy Spirit.' Gradually these views gained acceptance.

By 379, Theodosius, a strict Nicean, was Emperor. To establish unity in the Empire he sought closer links with the Bishop of Rome, Pope Damasus. In 381 Theodosius summoned the second World Council, the Ecumenical Council of Constantinople. The Nicene doctrine was there made the definition of Catholic orthodoxy, and the Catholic (Universal) Church of Christians was declared to be Trinitarian.

This 'orthodox trinitarian' Christianity was established by Theodosius as the only official religion of the Empire. He stated that all people under his rule were to live by the religion that "divine Peter, the Apostle, is said to have given to the Romans." They were to believe in " . . .one deity of the Father, Son and Holy Spirit with equal majesty in the Holy Trinity." (C.L. Manschrek, *A History of Christianity in the World*). Heretics and pagans were made subject to fines, all pagan temples were to be destroyed, and those who continued to offer pagan sacrifices were to be sentenced to death. All forms of Arianism were anathematised and Arius was posthumously condemned for denying the full divinity of the Word. Arianism had become a heresy.

In the eastern part of the Empire 'Nicene orthodoxy' was now firmly established, but in the West, Arianism, as a form of Christianity distinct from Catholicism, survived for about four hundred years.

By a strange turn of fate the saintly Ulfilas, who went as missionary to the barbarian Goths on the borders of the Black Sea, had been consecrated bishop in 360, at the time when semi-Arianism was the official Christianity of the Empire; and this was the religion he taught to the Gothic people. When they invaded and settled in the north western parts of the Empire, they brought their Arian Christianity with them, and the Visigoths and Ostrogoths took the heresy with them into Italy, Spain, North Africa and Gaul.

The Arian invaders were in constant conflict with the

Church of the Empire and the population whom they had conquered. By the sixth century, however, the Arian kingdoms had been absorbed into Catholicism, and by the eighth century Arianism, as an organised heretical form of Christianity, had disappeared. But the underlying conception of the Son as an intermediary distinct from the Father, never has. Many church-goers today understand their religion in this way. Some of the Protestant Churches, formed after the Reformation, were specifically based on the Arian, and therefore anti-Trinitarian, conception of Christ. The Unitarian churches (the word was first used in 1600), are an example of anti-Trinitarianism. For them Christ is a divinely inspired man, and not to be worshipped as God.

The Arian heresy, like many other heresies, was a catalyst in the formation of 'orthodox' doctrine. Credal statements about who Christ was, as Origen showed, were integral to an interpretation of Christianity. By the fourth century, after so many years of discussion and theorising, a final formula had become necessary. There had been two points at issue – if Christ were admitted not to be fully Divine, there could be no doctrine of the Incarnation; if Christ were said not to be fully human, there would be no doctrine of Redemption. Could a form of words reconcile these opposing ideas?

The creeds which had been used at baptism had varied slightly one from another in the different towns and districts of the Empire. At the Council of Constantinople, the Nicene formula was accepted and included in a creed to be used by the whole Church: "I believe in ... the Son of God ... of one substance with the Father, through whom all things are made." The 'Athanasian', or 'Nicene' Creed of 381 became the creed on which the present Roman Catholic, Anglican, and Orthodox Creeds are based.

As in the earlier baptismal creeds, there was the statement "who, for us men and for our salvation, came down from Heaven and was made man." In order to make completely clear the Trinitarian doctrine of the Church, there was added,

"I believe in the Holy Ghost, the Lord and Giver of Life, who proceedeth from the Father (and the Son – a later addition), who, with the Father and the Son together is worshipped and glorified, who spake through the prophets."

Arius, in his denial of the full divinity of Christ, had included denial of the divinity of the Spirit. There were others who went further and affirmed that the Holy Spirit was a Minister on the same level as the angels. (This was the Macedonian heresy, called after its founder, Macedonius.) The Nicene Creed established, once and for all, that in 'orthodox' Catholicism the three Persons of the Trinity were coequal in majesty and were one God.

No one has ever held that a logically defined and comprehensive statement of Christian religious philosophy has at any time been revealed or divinely expounded. The firmest upholders of belief in Divine Ordination agree that the Creed, as we know it, reached its present form after long, hard struggle and debate between churchmen.

Just as there seems to be an unanswerable problem in the existence of good and evil in the world, so there seems to be an irreconcilable contradiction between the omniscience and changelessness of God the Father, and the temptations and the suffering endured by God the Son, who grew from child to man. The words used in the Creed cannot *explain* St Hilary's 'invisible mysteries'; but what these statements affirm and, more especially, what they do not affirm, can be seen as giving direction to thought concerning 'orthodox' belief. Their most important aspect is their rejection of rationalisation and their retention of the 'mystery'. But can these credal statements be the fruit of a Divine Plan, notwithstanding the intellectual and political conflicts and compromises out of which they seemed to grow?

# X

# THE NESTORIANS

After the Council of Constantinople in 381, the Church's disputes still centred on the being of Christ. But now it was not the relation of the Son to the Father that occupied the minds of theologians, but the relation of Christ to man; that is, the relation of the human to the divine in Christ.

It was the churches in the eastern part of the Empire that attempted to elucidate this problem; the energies of the West were concentrated on its struggle with the barbarians. During the fourth and fifth centuries the two halves of the Empire were growing further and further apart. The Empire had divided into the Latin West and the Greek East. In fact, a petition sent to Rome during one of the fifth-century controversies was seriously delayed as no one in Rome could understand Greek. Ecclesiastical institutions, popular devotions, even the form of the liturgy were beginning to differ.

The position which Christianity occupied in daily life was also different. The Westerners had less time, or inclination, for abstract argument than the more urban and prosperous East. There, intellectual interest in doctrinal matters continued to dominate the minds of the citizens. No one took any notice of St Gregory Nazianzen's advice to the extremist Arians, who were proud of their clever use of syllogisms: "It was not given to everyone to discuss God, but only to those who had shown their capacity for it by advancing far enough on the way of perfection." (Gregory of Nazianzen, *Discourse* 27). The quarrels still went on.

Athanasius' affirmation that the Christian revelation depended on Christ being fully human and fully divine had been generally accepted. But the question that was now occupying the centre of debate was *how* was this so? In what manner was that which is God and that which is human united in Jesus Christ?

Among thinkers of that time some held that man was divided into body and soul; and some, with St Paul, that he was threefold – body, soul and spirit – 'soul' being the life-principle that he shared with all living beings, and 'spirit', that which was highest within him.

The Arians understood the Divine Word in Christ to be the vital principle that gives life to human beings. This was subject to change, and therefore inferior to the changeless God. This exposition went against the now 'orthodox' conception of Christ as the Second Person of the Trinity, and many felt that it must at all costs be refuted: among them, Apollinarius, Bishop of Laodicea in Syria, whose aim was to safeguard the Divinity and Unity of Christ.

Apollinarius was a firm supporter of the Nicene doctrine, but, a true Greek, he forced himself to face the intellectual difficulties involved. He knew that the Word, the Logos, consubstantial with God, had somehow in Christ to be united with his human nature assumed at the Incarnation. What was important for Apollinarius was to show how Christ, the Son, was truly God and yet that Jesus, who had the human nature of a man, was not two persons but one. The human nature was within a fleshly body and was, therefore, according to Apollinarius, subject to the possibility of sin. How could Christ be shown to be free from this possibility and perfect, as was God, and yet to have assumed humanity?

Apollinarius' answer was that, in Christ, the Logos took the place of our spirit. That being the case, his human nature was ruled by a Divine Guide, which meant that he would be forever sinless. Apollinarius thought that with this same argument, he had resolved the problem of uniting the divine and the human into one person. But he was immediately attacked. His opponents argued that, if the Logos took the place of the highest element in human nature, Christ was not complete man, since the highest human element had been left out. This meant that, according to the doctrine that Christ only healed and redeemed that which he had assumed, he could not be said to have redeemed the whole man. If Christ were not complete man, he was something else – neither God nor man – and the Incarnation was meaningless.

Apollinarius had many followers who supported his views, often exaggerating them or teaching different variations of them. Soon there were refutations of his teaching, and Pope Damusus condemned his errors and deposed him from his bishopric.

Apollinarianism was now a heresy, and edicts against it were issued at Rome, at Alexandria, at Antioch and at the Ecumenical Council of Constantinople; the Emperor Theodosius I also issued imperial ordinances against Apollinarianism and used the power of the secular law to suppress it. Apollinarianism, in fact, was never a serious threat to 'orthodoxy'. It is important because of the doctrines expounded in order to counteract it, which in their turn gave rise to a much more significant heresy.

At the beginning of the fifth century, the main theological attack against Apollinarianism came from the Church at Antioch. From the third century on there had been three great episcopal sees in the Empire – Rome, Alexandria and Antioch. Rome was growing in pre-eminence and gaining authority over the other sees. But from Rome there came no original body of philosophical or religious thought. The see of Rome merely assumed a magisterial attitude towards the theological controversies that were taking place in the Empire, in its role as capital city of the West, centre of government and recognised leader in the Church.

Alexandria was an immensely powerful see, partly because of its age-old reputation as a cosmopolitan centre of learning, and partly because of the great writers and Church leaders that it produced. Alexandrian intellectuals were strongly influenced by Plato, and Christianity was studied in the light of metaphysical philosophy. These Alexandrian thinkers tended to concentrate on the Divinity of Christ and described the Logos as a divine cosmic intermediary entering into our world. In their reading of the Old Testament, and even of the New, much was interpreted through allegory.

Antioch, the third great see, had a different reputation. From the days of its conversion it had been subjected to a more Semitic influence. Churchmen there were inclined to give more emphasis to moral teaching than to metaphysical speculation, and they aimed to keep in the forefront of their teaching the existence of an historical Christ. Their interpretation of the Bible tended to be literal, and allegory was viewed with suspicion.

Obviously, whole cities do not think exactly alike, but the names 'Alexandrian' and 'Antiochene', because of the general tendencies of their Church leaders, have been used as titles to describe two different schools of thought. The first described those who were concentrating on Christ as God; and the second those who, above all else, saw him as an historical human being. With these different emphases and approaches the Alexandrians and the Antiochenes were likely to take different sides in the Christological controversies.

Diodorus, Bishop of Tarsus, was an exponent of Antiochene Christology and attacked Apollinarius for downgrading the full humanity of Christ. He made the first explicit distinction between the Son of God and the Son of Mary in Jesus. His disciple was Theodore, Bishop of Mopsuesta. He, in turn, had as disciple the famous Nestorius, whose views were to cause so much division and upheaval in the Christian Church.

Theodore insisted on the existence of two completely separate natures in Christ. The two were united into a single 'someone' by conjunction. To retain Christ's full humanity he explained the Divinity within him as God's 'indwelling'. All people have the essence of God in them to give life, but only the worthy have the 'indwelling'. The 'indwelling' in Jesus

Christ was such that God, the Word, was the effective agent of all Jesus' actions, by virtue of the union of will between his divinity and his Man-hood. The emphasis here – and this was what Nestorius elaborated – was on Christ being 'Man who became God' rather than on 'God who became Man'.

The Nestorian controversy seems to have exploded into furious public debate largely because Nestorius was a violent, overbearing man, tactless in his expressions and misleading in his use of words. But much of what is attributed to him he may not explicitly have stated, and much of what was called Nestorianism was an almost immediate elaboration by his followers of what he had indeed stated.

Nestorius, as an Antiochene, considered that, if Christ were one person and divine, there would be a diminution of the human within him. The contraversialists from all sides made use of the words 'nature' and 'person'. By 'nature' they presumably meant 'the essential qualities of a thing . . . the innate disposition and character of a person,' as the O.E.D. has defined it, and, by 'person', 'an individual being'.

Nestorius' teaching appeared to show that there was a human person – Jesus of Nazareth – and a Divine person – the Word within Christ, and these distinct persons were united by unity of will – a moral union between two beings. Therefore the Son of God did not *become* a man, but was joined to a created man, born of the Virgin.

Over the years veneration for the Virgin Mary had been growing and was gradually being incorporated into public devotion. There is record of her title – 'Mother of God' – having been used in Egypt since the third century. Nestorius' reaction against this title arose partly from his Christological doctrine, and partly from his fear that she would be treated by Christian worshippers as a goddess – a return to paganism.

In 428 Nestorius had been summoned by the Emperor Theodosius II from his monastery near Antioch to become Patriarch of Constantinople. He was already a famous preacher and a zealous opponent of anything that seemed to him to border on heresy.

One of Nestorius' priests, in a sermon from the pulpit, declared that no one should call the Virgin Mary 'Mother of God', but should say 'Mother of Jesus'. This aroused serious protest, but Nestorius would not repudiate his assistant. He also refused to use the accepted word, *Theotokos* – the God-bearer. "Mary", he said, "only begot the man, in whom the Word is incarnate." (H. Daniel-Rops, *The Church in the Dark Ages*)

Cyril, theologian-bishop of the powerful See of Alexandria, wrote to admonish Nestorius, who firmly defended himself. Both appealed to Pope Celestine in Rome.

Cyril's Christology was theocentric, and the divinity of Christ had prime place in all his teaching. But he held that, in Christ, there was an indissoluble union between God and man. The Logos, incarnate in Christ, had taken on the charac-teristics of Man. This meant that Christ had the qualities of humanity in general, rather than those of an individual man.

The Pope was in agreement with Cyril, and opposed to Nestorius. With the Pope's blessing, Cyril set out twelve propositions explaining his doctrine, which Nestorius was to accept on pain of anathema; Nestorius refused. The Pope summoned a Council at Rome in 430 which condemned Nestorius' theses. Again Nestorius refused to retract. Cyril then anathematised him, and Nestorius persuaded the Emperor Theodosius to call a council to settle the dispute.

A Council was summoned at Ephesus in 431. The city mob demonstrated violently against the 'opponents of the Mother of God'. The Emperor intervened, and, at one time during the proceedings, imprisoned both Cyril *and* Nestorius. Church-men condemned each other; the common people rioted; the Imperial civil servants carried on intrigues between both par-ties. Finally, Theodosius dismissed the Council saying, quite rightly, that it had failed to achieve reconciliation. But Nes-torius himself was condemned as a heretic, deposed and exiled.

The Emperor tried to bring the divided parties together and, in 433, mutual concessions were made between Cyril of

Alexandria and John of Antioch, Nestorius' supporter. John agreed to the condemnation of Nestorius, and Cyril to part of a credo drawn up by John, using the words, 'consubstantial with us in humanity'. Nestorianism, as a heresy within the Empire, was conquered, but the compromise left extremists on both sides unsatisfied, and disputes continued.

Many Nestorians fled persecution and settled in Persia and Syria, where they founded churches. From there, in the next two centuries, they went as missionaries all over Asia, from Arabia to China.

Though Nestorianism as a school of thought ceased to exist in the fifth century, there are still Nestorian Churches in Iraq and Iran. The only indigenous Christian churches in Iran today are Nestorian; though small in number, the Nestorian communities form complete villages and are closely united. But these surviving Nestorian churches show no signs of possessing a heretical creed. They seem rather to have developed different customs and rituals, as a result of their long separation from mainstream Christianity, and through the influence of the country in which they are living.

It seems that Nestorianism, as a school of thought, never had a clearly defined system of heretical doctrine. Its importance lies less in what might have been, had a different line been taken at the councils, than in the effect that the controversy had on the history of the Church. As in the case of other combats with 'heresy', it led to a further definition of dogma by the Church: that of indissoluble union between God and man.

The opposing arguments of the Nestorians and the anti-Nestorians were abstruse and complicated, but many of the Nestorian statements about Christ, taken by themselves, at first seemed helpful to their hearers. It was the logical development of these statements, as elaborated by the disputants, that gave rise to doctrinal difficulties.

If the Pope and Councils had decided differently it is possible that the adoption of Nestorianism could have led to

Christ being regarded in 'orthodox' teaching simply as a man, though one inspired to a superlative degree by the indwelling Logos. This might have caused Christ to be revered purely as a great teacher and example. There is a tendency today towards this kind of thinking, but the religious atmosphere of the fifth century was on the whole not congenial to such a mode of thought. Christianity was then held to be primarily a belief in a cosmic system of salvation, so that the adoption of Nestorian Christology would not necessarily have led to a 'humanitarian' view of Christ.

The Nestorian heresy was important for the divisions it created within the Church of the Eastern Empire – divisions which it caused and which were exacerbated by the heresy that arose as a reaction to it. This latter heresy – Monophysitism – was to create a schism in the Church, to disrupt the Empire, and to give rise to separated Eastern churches that still exist today – the Churches of the Monophysites in Egypt and Abyssinia.

Out of the intellectual conflicts concerning both these heresies – Nestorianism and Monophysitism – came the formula which became 'orthodox' Catholic doctrine on the nature of Christ. This formula was accepted at the Council of Chalcedon in 451. But before final agreement was reached, the Monophysite heresy had also to be dealt with.

Eutyches, the superior of a monastery near Constantinople, put forward an extreme anti-Nestorian doctrine. He emphasised the Godhead in Christ to the point of denying his humanity. He used the phrase, "One incarnate nature of God the Word", in order to explain that, at the Incarnation, the two natures of God and of man blended into one, so that they became one nature, fully divine. Jesus was *homoousion* with the Father, but not with mankind. This doctrine of the One Divine Nature was sometimes called Eutychianism, or, more usually, Monophysitism.

This over emphasis on Divinity aroused suspicion of heresy among Church leaders in Constantinople, and Eutyches was condemned at a Synod there in 448, presided over by Flavian, Bishop of Constantinople. Eutyches managed to persuade the Emperor, Theodosius II, to summon a council to rehear his case. Theodosius agreed, and so, in 449, the notorious 'Robber Council' met at Ephesus. This council sunk to new depths of appalling behaviour.

The Pope, Leo I, had written a letter to Bishop Flavian defining in lucid terms what, in the West, was held to be 'orthodox' doctrine on the Being of Christ. At the 'Robber Council', this important letter, known as the 'Tome of Leo', was refused a hearing amidst a tumultuous uproar. Bishops threatened each other with death; the mob rioted; Bishop Flavian was so maltreated that he died, and the Bishop of Alexandria (Cyril's successor) excommunicated the leaders of Antioch and the Pope himself!

At this time, each of the two halves of the Roman Empire had an Emperor, and the Emperor of the West, Valentinius III, joined with the Pope to annul the Council's decrees. Temporary peace came with the death of Theodosius in 480. He had supported the recalcitrant bishops and their allies, but the new Emperor and Empress of the East were loyal to the Pope.

In 451, the fourth Ecumenical Council was summoned at Chalcedon. Six hundred bishops, mostly from the East, attended, as well as two papal legates. Finally, the 'Robber Council's' proceedings were annulled. Eutyches was declared a heretic; Monophysitism and Nestorianism were both condemned as heresies. The 'Tome of Leo' was approved and, as will be seen, accepted as the basis for orthodox Christological belief.

Despite the agreement at the Council of Chalcedon disputes and quarrels about the nature of Christ continued throughout the Eastern Empire until the seventh century and the Arab invasion. Emperors changed sides between Monophysites and anti-Monophysites and many bishops changed sides according to who was Emperor.

Between 484 and 519 there was schism between Constantinople and Rome. Popes were imprisoned and anti-Popes installed, supporters of rival bishops fought each other, and separate Monophysite Churches were established in Egypt, Ethiopia and Syria.

By the seventh century, the quarrels between Nestorian Christians and Monophysite Christians had spread all over Asia Minor and North Africa. Mohammed, who originally had had sincere leanings towards Christianity, was horrified at the disunity among Christians and felt that he was called to lead not only the pagan Arabs, but also these betrayers of their faith, back to the Religion of Unity. Certainly, the squabbling Christian churches were no bulwark against the oncoming pressure of Islam.

In the eastern part of the Roman Empire the Christological disputes were not settled until the sixth Ecumenical Council in 680, when Monothelitism, which was a doctrine maintaining a single Divine Will in Christ, and a daughter-heresy to Monophysitism, was finally contained. In that Council of Constantinople, it was stated that, just as there were two distinct Natures in Christ, so there were two distinct Wills, one human and one Divine. The decision of this council marked the end of the Christological controversies. Too late, the disputants realised that they must end their struggles and attempt to defend themselves against the Islamic invaders.

Monophysitism had split into innumerable schools and sects, each more abstruse than the last; but the quarrels were, by the end of the fifth century, largely connected with politics – Rome versus Constantinople, Antioch versus Alexandria, the Imperial Court versus rising nationalism – so that religious and doctrinal ideas tended to disappear. The importance of Monophysitism in connection with the formation of 'orthodox' dogma virtually ceased after the Council of Chalcedon in 451. Nevertheless, Monophysite ideas had a significant influence on the theology of the Eastern Christian Church and, through the East, on all Christians.

The Monophysites, when the controversy began, were an

intensely religious and pious section of the community, many of them tending towards a mystical type of religion. And despite the political and theological squabbles that were disfiguring the Church, the sixth century was the age of the great spiritual writers from the Eastern Monasteries, and of the blossoming of Byzantine religious art.

The greatest of the Byzantine mystics was a Syrian, who used the name of 'Dionysius the Areopagite' (the Athenian disciple of St Paul); his writings influenced Christian thinkers and contemplatives throughout the Middle Ages. He wrote of the Godhead as "The Divine Darkness that is beyond light – a 'Something' beyond goodness, beyond being, transcending all human thought." (C. Dawson, *The Making of Europe*) In his writings, Dionysius describes how Life and Power from this ineffable Divine Source are transmitted to mankind through descending hierarchies of heavenly ministers – a doctrine reminiscent of the Gnostics. Many Eastern Churchmen, who were attracted towards Monophysitism, had studied such ideas. To them, the Incarnation could only be understood as the appearance on earth of Divine Power, clothed in human form.

The emphasis given to the Divinity of Christ increased the sense of awe and mystery in Christianity, which is such a powerful ingredient of Byzantine Art. And this sense of awe and mystery entered into the Western Church from the Church in the East. But, because of this emphasis, Western Church leaders feared that the doctrine of the human, historical Christ might tend to be forgotten. By overlooking Christ's humanity, the Christian religion, it was thought, would be distorted. If Christ had not been a fully human being, living in historical time, where was the 'Good News' for humanity – its at-one-ment with God? Where was the perfect acceptance of suffering and death? What was the point of Christ's temptation and what the point of his suffering?

The purpose of Pope Leo's credal statement in the 'Tome of Leo' (his epistle to Bishop Flavian) was to guard against this danger in Monophysitism and, at the same time, prevent the extremes of Nestorianism.

The fundamental assertion in the creed based on this 'Tome of Leo' was expressed in these terms: " . . .there is to be confessed one and the same Son, our Lord Jesus Christ, perfect in Godhead and perfect in Manhood, truly God and truly man, of rational soul and body, of the same substance with the Father according to the Godhead, and of the same substance with us according to the manhood, like to us in all respects, without sin, begotten of the Father before all time according to the Godhead; in these latter days for us and for our salvation, born of the Virgin Mary, the Mother of God, according to the manhood, one and the same Christ, Son, Lord, Only-begotten, in two natures, unconfusedly, immutably, indivisibly, inseparately, the distinction of being by no means taken away by the union, but rather the peculiarity of each nature being preserved and concurring in one person and one substance, not parted or separated into two persons, but one and the same Son and Only-begotten, divine Word, the Lord Jesus Christ; as from the beginning the prophets declared concerning him, and the Lord Jesus Christ has taught us, and the creed of the holy fathers has transmitted to us."

This was the creed accepted at the Council of Chalcedon and it was this affirmation that became, from then on, the 'orthodox' Christian doctrine on the nature of Christ. Nevertheless, disputes and disruptions were to continue well into the seventh century.

It might seem strange that the ordinary citizenry should become so inflamed with fury about abstruse theological issues that it could be transformed into a rioting mob; and strange, too, that rival bands, shouting rival religious slogans, could have fought each other under the banner of their particular theological school and doctrinal definition. But there has always been a collective need to find a focus for crowd emotion. In this context, there is not very much difference between nationalism and football, political ideology and religious

doctrine. The crowds in the Eastern Roman Empire marched
for their bishop and his party. They liked marching then as
people like marching now.

The expression of strongly held ideas can, in the course of
debate, degenerate into violent emotional conflict. The majority of people today, as in the past, tend to regard ideas,
especially religious ones, as their own personal property. They
are particularly possessive about their conceptions of 'God'
and the relation of 'God' to 'man' – hence the heat in religious
discussions, even on a social level. When these 'possessions'
are 'owned' by a group, the heat is, of course, increased. 'God'
exists in such and such a way, or does not exist at all, whatever
x or y believe. But somehow x and y think that they must fight
to prove the validity of their ideas: not just because they are
angry at opposition, but in order to defend or attack 'God'.
Today, religious labels among warring communities are inextricably interwoven with politics and with political rights.
In an age when religion rather than politics was the predomi-
nant concern, it was arguments about abstract definitions
rather than about political rights that were liable to bring about
the fighting.

The exponents of the various doctrines continued to work
out their theoretical conclusions, which grew more and more
complicated and seemed to have less and less relevance to what
is generally held to be Christianity. History has shown that
extremism and exaggeration in the exposition of an idea have
often given rise to a 'heresy'. Orthodoxy, at Chalcedon, per-
formed its role of keeping the balance between exaggerations.
It was constantly necessary for the Church to keep a right
emphasis, so that concentration on one aspect of what was
taught did not lead to neglect or distortion of the rest. The
Church's credal formulation at Chalcedon was balanced and
comprehensive, and maintained the importance of both aspects
of teaching on Christ. This meant that an orthodox Christian
must not regard Christ simply as a supremely good man and
teacher, nor simply as the Divine Logos, beyond the confines

of humanity. But though the theory that contained the two conceptions had been lucidly stated, such words probably solved little for those sincerely trying to discover meaning for themselves. A clear-cut logical statement had to be issued in order to put an end to conflict, but how much value have such statements towards the understanding of a Mystery? Is there not a danger that lucid expositions may lead those who accept them into believing that they understand, and so need venture no further?

# XI

# PELAGIUS

There is one more major heresy to be considered before it can be said that the doctrines of Christianity took their final form – the form in which they are generally recognised today. This heresy is called Pelagianism. It was a heresy of the Western Empire, and was a different type of heresy from those previously discussed. At no time was there any sign of a separate school or sect, and there was certainly no danger of a separated church being formed. In a sense, there was not even a question as to whether the ideas in dispute were or were not what Christ had taught, or were or were not what had been revealed. The defenders of 'orthodoxy' were only fearful of what might be the outcome, if certain 'heteredox' ideas were to be generally accepted and theologically developed. It is possible that, had this happened, Christian doctrines might have undergone a change; but, strangely, the controversy over Pelagianism appears to have been more of a contrast between two fundamental attitudes, rather than a conflict between theological theories or beliefs. Its importance lies in the depth of its questions and in the influence of these questions on Christian thinkers and reformers of succeeding centuries, rather than in its bearing on what Christianity did become or what it might have been.

The Pelagian dispute did not arouse such fierce antagonisms among the people as did the disputes in the Eastern Empire. The Latins were less speculative and more practical in their approach to religion; their attention was primarily focussed on facing external dangers.

The bishops and theologians in the West, who were expounding Christian doctrine, concentrated on a different aspect of Christianity from those in the East. While the Eastern theologians were struggling with problems connected with the nature of Christ and with the meaning of the Trinity, Latin churchmen of the West were disputing over difficulties that more directly concerned the nature of man and the Christian life. The East "laid stress on the supernatural character of Christianity as a fact of the objective world, and developed the doctrines of the Trinity and the Incarnation"; the West "emphasised the supernatural character of Christianity as an agency in the subjective world, and developed the doctrine of Sin and Grace." (*Encyclopaedia Britannica*).

Whether or not Free Will existed in man, how much his choice of action was his own or was predetermined, were the questions at the centre of the doctrinal disputes in the West. As in the case of all expositions of belief that came to be considered heretical, fundamental questions, not hitherto investigated, were brought into the open. They were then seen to raise a serious problem, and one in need of solution. Doctrines to settle the problem had to be formulated – in this instance, the doctrines concerning 'Sin' and 'Grace'. In order to understand the development of these doctrines, it is necessary to go back in history to the beginning of the fifth century.

Pelagius, the originator of the controversy, came to Rome from Britain. Not very much is known about his early life. It seems, from what he subsequently wrote, that he wanted to enter monastic life, but that his father was against this. Pelagius lived the ascetic life of a monk and was often called 'monk' by his contemporaries, but he never joined a monastic order. He abjured the title of 'monk', and maintained that the office of teacher was open to all, for a teacher was what he aspired to be. He wanted to encourage laymen to instruct one another in the Faith. Though he held that the calling of a cleric was a high and noble one, he saw no moral difference between a clerical and a lay vocation. He emphasised this because, since Constantine's recognition of Christianity, many of the clergy had come to see themselves as a superior and exclusive section of the community. Pelagius argued that moral responsibility belonged to all Christians.

When he arrived in Rome Pelagius was horrified at the laxity and low level of morality that he found there. It seemed to him that excuses for this were being made on the ground that weakness was an inevitable part of the human condition. In his preaching his first object was to remove what he saw as a stumbling block to effort. He wished to show that human beings were *not* powerless, and he aimed to revitalise the struggle against sinfulness.

"If I ought, then I can," was the motto he used, therefore insisting on human freedom of will to choose. God's grace was there to help all to salvation, but man must make himself worthy of it by striving. Pelagius insisted that we are ourselves able to do all that God commands: "Where the will is not absolutely free, there is no sin." This conception of man's will was based on the theory that, at each moment of volition, no matter what came before, the will is in equipoise, able to choose good or evil.

Pelagius was a moralist, not a theologian, and his emphasis was on exhortation, not on doctrine. In fifth-century intellectual circles theoretical Christian doctrine was being given more importance than practical Christian ethics. Pelagius was determined to remedy this.

To the modern reader, these teachings of Pelagius would seem to be, not only blameless, but constructive; and at first they were treated in that light, and aroused no opposition.

In 410, Alaric, leader of the Western Goths, invaded and sacked Rome. Pelagius, with his companions and assistants, took refuge in Africa. There one of his supporters, a lawyer named Coelestius, publicly preached, clarified and elaborated on Pelagius' views. In Coelestius' explanation it appeared that human nature was not inherently sinful. Adam's sin had injured only himself, not the whole human race. Adam gave an example to sin that led to imitation, not a taint to be inherited

by all. Every child, therefore, was born with power to choose
the right. Man, if he chose rightly, could live without sin, and
this even before the advent of Christ.

In the eyes of the 'orthodox', Coelestius had denied the
existence of 'original sin', the need for infant baptism, and
even the efficacy of the Incarnation and Death of Christ. On
these grounds Coelestius was refused the ordination he sought,
and the name of Pelagius was associated with him in this
suspicion of heresy.

At this time Pelagius had already left for Palestine, where his
teaching was attacked, by, among others, Jerome, the great
translator of the Bible. A synod at Jerusalem referred the
matter to the Pope. Meanwhile, another Synod at Lydda fully
exonerated Pelagius. The following year, however, he was
condemned at the Council of Carthage in 416, and Pope
Innocent I confirmed the condemnation. But the succeeding
Pope, Zosimus, retracted this and declared Pelagius to be
orthodox and blameless, stating that, if the essential Faith was
kept, the rest was unprofitable disputation. Nevertheless, the
Pope was wavering. Orthodox Churchmen now appealed to
the Emperor Honorius, saying that there was disorder in
Rome and in Palestine. The power of the State was invoked,
and the Emperor declared Pelagius and Coelestius to be heretics and liable to punishment. In 418, a plenary council of all
Africa reasserted the verdict of the previous Pope. Pope
Zosimus now made up his mind and sent a letter excommuni-
cating Pelagius.

Pelagius, who throughout these events desired above all to
remain orthodox and who had no wish to found a heretical
school, finally left Palestine. He died ignored and forgotten.
His followers continued to spread his ideas but, in 431, at the
Council of Ephesus, Pelagianism (together with Nestorianism)
was condemned as a heresy.

Pelagius would not have elaborated his views, nor developed them into an intellectual system, if it had not been for the
attacks on his preaching – above all, the attacks made by his

greatest antagonist, St Augustine, then Bishop of Hippo. St Augustine saw more clearly than anyone what were the ultimate implications of Pelagius' teaching in relation to doctrines now held to be central to 'orthodox' Christianity – the doctrines concerned with original sin and the fall of man.

The story of the fall of man in *Genesis,* which gave an explanation of how sin and death entered a world created by an infinitely good God, was made an essential part of Christian teaching on salvation. Except for St Paul, St Augustine was the first to give a precise definition of this doctrine. How far Adam's story was then taken by Christians to be literal fact is not clear. (The Alexandrian School would certainly have treated it as an allegory.) The importance of the doctrine, however, does not lie there, but in the acceptance of the belief in an inherited human corruption – that by nature, we tend towards evil rather than good.

Augustine attacked Pelagius' views, and his attacks grew more intense as the controversy continued. Yet through it all he never ceased to have the highest regard for Pelagius as a person, and continued to speak of him with affection and respect. He praised his "... zeal, indeed, for God", and applauded his "... noble character and pure living. Here was a good man, who should be spoken of on all sides." (Augustine, *De Peccatorum Meritus*).

Pelagius himself had great veneration for St Augustine and right to the end, longed to be reconciled with him. But Pelagius and Augustine differed profoundly in nature and experience.

St Augustine's writings are great, not only because of the power of his intellect, but because even the most philosophical of his works were rooted in his own spiritual and emotional experience. They grew from his inner life. Pelagius had not experienced the intense realisation of his own weakness, which came to St Augustine with his conversion to Christianity. For Pelagius, the centre of Christianity was moral striving towards perfection; for Augustine, it was abandonment to God. Because of his 'puritanical' character Pelagius had little understanding of this side of Christianity; to him, St Augustine's conception savoured of moral feebleness.

In St Augustine's *Confessions,* a book much read at that time, there was a prayer: "Give what You command, command what You will." To Pelagius this seemed an encouragement to lazy passivity and to the abandonment of self-reliance. His reaction to this prayer caused him to intensify his preaching against the moral sloth that he found all around him. Pelagius saw the central dogmatic issue to be whether or not it is possible for a man to live without sin. He maintained that it was not necessary to his argument to be able to point to a completely sinless man in history; what was important for him, was that it must be possible for people, of their own volition, to live without sin. God commanded this, he said, and He would not command the impossible.

Pelagius' emphatic assertion that man, living on this earth, can be completely sinless and must use his own will-power to achieve this, was part of his evangelical preaching – encouragement to Christian people to improve their lives. He had not realised that his description of how a Christian should live would call into question some fundamental Christian dogmas, and raise intractable problems concerning 'man's free will.'

At first sight, the 'orthodox', in their condemnation of Coelestius and in their attacks on Pelagius during the synods of Jerusalem and Carthage, appear to be narrow, literal interpreters of dogma, denouncing sensible, open-minded thinkers. Coelestius and Pelagius were attacked for holding that the sin of Adam did not condemn the human race to inevitable sinfulness, that unbaptised infants were not automatically damned, and that the human race does not die because of Adam nor rise again because of Christ. But St Augustine's works, refuting the ideas of Pelagius, show that these attacks led to deeper issues, developing into theories of philosophical and religious importance. And St Augustine was a committed defender of 'orthodoxy' – an upholder of Catholic tradition as the one link, via the Apostles, with the original Christian revelation.

In the Pelagian controversy, continuing argument and counter-argument led St Augustine into such emphatic expression of his views that they finally developed into doctrines of intolerable harshness. Yet, even at his most extreme, St Augustine's writings reveal a mystical, theocentric conception of Christianity. He embraced seeming contradictions and paradoxes, in contrast with the rationalist, humanitarian approach of his opponent.

From the experience of his own life St Augustine had complete conviction that, by himself, he was unable to escape from what he held to be his most damaging sins, however much he might desire to do so. He believed that it was the grace of God alone that set him free from them. So in any philosophical dispute about 'sin', 'grace' and 'free will', St Augustine wrote not only from the basis of accepted doctrine, but from what he had observed in himself to be a fact.

When Pelagius was exonerated at the Synod of Lydda, and it seemed that he had retracted anything that might be of a heterodox nature, St Augustine was overjoyed; Pelagius was declared once more to be in communion with the Catholic Church. But Augustine had misgivings that all was not as straightforward as it might appear; and he was right.

Pelagius continued to maintain that the issues between him and his opponents were not of a dogmatic nature, but were legitimate differences of opinion over a specific point. So although he had no desire to rebel against 'orthodoxy', he again began to write. His ideas were spreading – human beings, by their own volition, can and should make the first step towards belief and faith in God and in Christ, they can, by their own will, choose to obey.

It was specifically to refute these affirmations that Augustine had entered the controversy. Those, he said, who hold that man can live righteously from his own nature alone, make the Cross of Christ to be of no effect; though human nature had been created without blemish, it was corrupted by the Sin of Adam. Adam deliberately sinned through pride – the belief that his own will was to be followed, not that of God. The tendency to sin was then passed on to Adam's descendants. So all have sinned in Adam, as well as of themselves, and can be redeemed only by Christ, by his free gift, not by their own merit.

Augustine maintained that Pelagius had put salvation outside Christ and his Church; that, for Pelagius, Christ was merely an example, not a Saviour; so that man was not dependent on Christ's grace. This meant that human beings, through their own volition and power, could follow Christ – a proposition Augustine strongly denied. He held that man could do nothing without prior grace, which he termed 'prevenient grace'. It was this grace which enabled men to turn to God and to believe in Christ; without that initial grace, there would be no hope.

The argument here centred round the doctrine of original sin. As Pelagius' ideas developed and became more systematised, it appeared that in the Pelagian explanation of the Fall, sin was held not to be a generic taint, but a quality in individual actions. Adam did not bring sin into the world – but was the first sinner. In fact, he did not hand on an evil taint, but an evil example.

In this explanation of Original Sin (which is, in effect, the denial of it) there could be no doctrine of mankind's common need for redemption and, therefore, no doctrine of cosmic atonement. Pelagius was probably drawn into the position of denying the concept of original sin by his fervent opposition to the belief, which had crept into 'orthodox' theology, that subject to Christian baptism, mankind was redeemed in its entirety. Wishing to give primacy to the ethics, rather than to the metaphysics of Christianity, he claimed that there was no universality of sin, and therefore no universality of salvation. Grace could come at any time to any person.

In St Augustine's teaching on grace, the root sin inherited from Adam was the tendency to sin; having inherited this tendency, man was unable of himself to turn to God. But the perfect obedience of Christ annulled Adam's disobedience – a representative of the human race had achieved perfection. Christ's free gift of grace enabled those who received it to escape the inherited taint and to strive towards God. Through the Church, which dispensed grace by means of the Sacraments, man could come to salvation. Christ was the Saviour of the World in the sense that he came to give saving grace to those in the world whom God had chosen. These elect were chosen to receive the gift of 'prevenient grace'; they were given the grace of perseverance, so that they could continue in repentance and finally reach blessedness. Those who were not chosen to receive grace, could do nothing.

This argument appeared to postulate an unjust God, who arbitrarily decided to choose a few for reward and to condemn the rest to punishment. The Pelagians reacted strongly against a doctrine with such implications.

In the process of debate these implications in St Augustine's teaching were given logical expression, and his later followers further exaggerated them. But St Augustine had also insisted that it is what you are rather than what you do that is fundamental; no one could know whether he or any one else was a 'chosen one'.

It can be understood from St Augustine's sermons and from his expositions of the Psalms that the very fact of striving towards God implies the reception of His grace; the very fact of perseverance in striving shows that grace is being given; thus, in life, as against theory, the harsh doctrine of planned prevenient grace should have little practical importance.

This doctrine was important to St Augustine because it described a God-centred, not a man-centred universe and emphasised the redeeming Christ of the Atonement, rather than a Christ seen only as a human example and a wise teacher. Augustine's main contention was that if human nature could achieve eternal life unaided, faith in Christ was needless.

The question of the inherited taint – the barrier between God and man – led also to disputes over infant baptism. All Christians of Pelagius' time, including the Pelagians themselves, agreed that infant baptism was necessary. But the Pelagians, holding that new-born children were born free from original sin, regarded their baptism as a form of higher sanctification – an entrance into glory, not a means of salvation. To bring themselves more into line with 'orthodoxy', the Pelagians added that infants had the 'capacity to sin' and therefore also needed baptism on that account.

St Augustine and the 'orthodox' held that the grace given at baptism was essential for washing away the taint of original sin and was therefore essential for gaining salvation. Though the logical outcome of this view appeared to be that infants who died unbaptised were damned, St Augustine wrote in a letter to Jerome, "When the question of children is raised, it troubles me sorely. I assure you, and I am at a loss what to answer." (*Dutch Roman Catholic Catechism*). And since later theologians appear to have been equally at a loss the question was shelved.

St Augustine's teaching on prevenient grace, given by God according to His pre-ordained plan, was developed by his followers after his death, into a doctrine of predestination. This aroused opposition, particularly in the monasteries, as it seemed to nullify all personal striving for self-denial and virtue. Anti-Augustinianism grew, and this school of thought became known as Semi-Pelagianism.

St John Cassian of Marseilles, founder of monasteries in southern Gaul, was one of the chief exponents of Semi-Pelagian teaching. He had been a deacon of one of the Fathers of the Greek Church, the great St John Chrysostum, Patriarch of Constantinople. From him he accepted the teaching that God's grace and man's free will worked together. He disagreed with Pelagius that man, by nature was incorrupt. He held that man was essentially sinful, but with a spark of good within which could lead him to desire God's grace. The gift of grace was necessary for conversion, but people could turn to God of their own volition to receive it. God bestowed grace on all who sought it, although He sometimes bestowed it without it being sought.

The 'orthodox' attacked these ideas on the grounds that they still gave man and not God the credit for his own salvation. The arguments continued. Finally, at a Synod held at Orange in 529, the Church made a definitive pronouncement on Pelagianism and Semi-Pelagianism; both were condemned.

The official doctrine of 'orthodox' Christianity now stated that man inherits a nature so corrupt that he has no power to turn to God unless Divine grace comes to him first. Grace inspires the desire for baptism; it does not elect souls, for all who are baptised are capable of salvation. So although the desire for baptism is inspired by grace, there is no question of a pre-ordained elect. All baptised souls are able to attain blessedness, if they 'labour faithfully'. Those who insisted that man's own will could anticipate God's gift of grace, which alone could bring about his conversion, were condemned. And, conversely, so were those who taught that anyone could be predestined to wrongdoing and separation from God.

The 'orthodox' decision, as in so many previous instances, was formulated in a moderate statement, avoiding extremes. But once again the fundamental question was left unsolved; and the antithesis between a foreknown and fore-ordained Divine Plan, and man's free will and freedom of choice was not explained. There might not have been such an 'either-or' formulation of the problem if St Augustine's other writings had been taken into account.

The word 'will' in relation to man can be understood in different ways. Pelagius posited that a human being is able to choose between good and evil at any moment, no matter what came before. For Pelagius, the 'will' meant the power of choice, unbiased and neutral. Augustine describes our wills as already conditioned by previous happenings. In *De Civitate Dei,* he writes "But it does not follow that nothing should be left to our free will, because God knows the certain and set order of all causes, (for, our very wills are in that order of causes, which God knows so surely and has in His prescience), since human wills are the (immediate) causes of all human action."

According to St Augustine our wills at each moment are not neutral, but better or worse as a result of what has come before. But they exist on a different scale from that which causes them to be as they are. "Without the use of scales and levels, things are thought of as opposites when they are not so." (Maurice Nicoll, *The Mark*). It is impossible for the mind to relate its conception of the growth of life in the Universe to the actual life of a particular person. One cannot say, "If there is a foreknown plan in the Universe, therefore all my actions are predetermined." The scales are too different for such a conclusion to make sense.

Human minds cannot contain concepts of very different scales at one and the same time. "It is impossible to conceive a chair in the planetary world." (P.D. Ouspensky, *A New Model of the Universe*). A chair has a function in a different-sized world. The same applies when thinking in terms of an individual person in relation to the cosmic order. Confusion of scale brings contradiction into thinking.

In the same way, St Augustine's study of time emphasises the need to think according to scale, and has a bearing on the antithesis between Divine foreknowing and the Divine commandment, laid on man, to choose and then to act rightly. In the *Confessions,* St Augustine questioned what we mean by 'time'. He concluded that our 'time' – our movement from the past, through the present, to the future – is a man-made conception, our 'time' coming into existence, when *we* came into existence. But he says, "In the Eternal, nothing passeth, but the whole is present." If our minds were capable of comprehending the difference between these scales the apparent contradictions would disappear.

St Augustine's description of the true freedom, which is

different from Pelagius' 'freedom of indifference', also intro-
duces another dimension. He held that true freedom – our
wills being purified from their weaknesses – would be freedom
not to sin; freedom from what corrupts us. This true freedom
means participation in God's Freedom.

St Augustine is speaking on a different level from Pelagius,
and the essence of his case against him can be summed up in
this quotation from his *De Spiritu et Littera:* "Why should
miserable men venture to pride themselves on their free will
before they are set free?"

The argument over what constitutes free will and how
much we have the power of free choice continued throughout
the subsequent history of Christianity. To what extent human
beings are free to choose and to what extent they are predetermined were questions central to Calvinism at the time of
the Reformation. And whether true faith alone can bring
salvation, and how much meritorious works are necessary to
salvation were questions at the heart of Lutheranism. It would
be interesting to know which side St Augustine would have
taken had he lived in the sixteenth century.

Most Christian people today, if questioned about their
ideas, would feel it important to say that we possess the power
to turn to God and to aim at doing right; and they would
probably say, as St John Cassian had taught, that the essence of
Christianity is in the co-operation of human will and God's
grace. In fact, most present-day Christians are more Semi-
Pelagian than Augustinian, however much St Augustine may
have striven to uphold the 'orthodox' tradition of the Great
Church.

But the outcome of the Pelagian controversy was important, not because there was any 'decision' made between the
doctrine of free will and that of fore-ordained grace, but
because it contributed to the stabilising of Christian doctrine.

The Trinity had already been theologically defined. Jesus
Christ had long been worshipped as Son of God; and the Son
of God was affirmed to be coequal with God. Now it was

clearly stated that because of original sin, the depth of man's fallen state was such that it necessitated redemption by God Himself. Man is not self-sufficient; his own reasoning and his own will-power alone, cannot rescue him. The central theme of Christianity was thus formally established: the Second Person of the Blessed Trinity became Incarnate as a man in order to achieve Atonement and to bring Divine grace, which is not merited, but without which we can do nothing.

By the end of the fifth century the basic tenets of mainstream Christianity had been formed and its doctrines expressed in the same way as they are today. But the Pelagian controversy is not dead. More insistent than ever are the arguments concerning our freedom of choice, or the lack of it.

# XII

## THE CHURCH OF ROME

The point has now been reached – the end of the fifth century –
when the Catholic Church had become generally accepted as
the one true vehicle of Christianity. Whatever impacts and
influences had or had not affected the development of its
doctrine, the leaders of the Great Church were firm in their
conviction that its prime duty was to preserve its vital link
with Christianity's founder, and that it was fulfilling this duty.

By the end of the fifth century it had become clear who was
the head of this Church, and so who had the final voice in the
declaration of 'orthodox' doctrine. Acceptance of this final
voice itself became part of 'orthodoxy'.

For the next thousand years this acceptance, at any rate in
theory, formed the basis of Western Christendom, but questions were still asked, as they had been from the beginning.
Was the establishment of an institutional Church part of the
original Christian teaching? Was an organised Church, headed
by a supreme arbiter of truth, already implicit in the birth of
Christianity? Some of the early heresies had questioned the
very need for an organised Church at all. Nevertheless, by the
beginning of the sixth century, the Great Church, with a
supreme arbiter at its head, was recognised by the majority of
Christians as the one true guardian of Christian tradition, and
the one true teacher of the Christian religion. Though it can
give no definitive answer to the 'heretic's' questions, history
can describe how this came to be so.

The *ecclesia,* (the 'assembly' – translated as 'Church'), at first
denoted only Christian believers in Jerusalem. This was recorded in *Acts*. As the preaching of the Gospel spread,

communities were established in Asia Minor also. Paul and
Barnabas, after their first missionary journey, returned to
Antioch and, as is stated in *Acts* xiv 27, called together the
'church' there, that it might hear of their experiences.

In the days of St Paul the elders of the local *ecclesiae* appointed
members of their communities to distribute alms to the needy
brethren. Gradually this custom became general. Each community had its group of church officers. The 'elder' had
become 'bishop', supported by a 'presbyter' and a 'deacon'.
An epistle of St Ignatius of Antioch, at the end of the first
century, shows this to be the case, certainly in Asia Minor. So
an organisation of church officials developed, whose function
was to administer local church affairs and to instruct the
people.

The formation of a central Church, uniting these individual
local churches, was hastened by the growth of the second-
century heresies. It was necessary for those who were opposing these heresies to show that there was a community in
existence possessing the true Apostolic doctrine. Irenaeus used
the conception of unbroken Apostolic succession as a weapon
to combat the heretics.

Irenaeus' statement of ideas gained general acceptance; the
apostles had been instructed by Christ; they appointed elders
as their successors, who, in their turn, appointed their successors, and so on in a continuous line. Thus, the original teaching would be preserved and transmitted without error. A
unified, institutional Church, therefore, was seen to be essential for guarding and handing on to future generations the
truths of the Christian religion. An organised Church was
regarded, not only as a necessary institution for governing the
whole Christian community, but as the link with the original
revelation.

By the end of the second century it was universal practice for
a bishop to be head of the local church and, at first, each small
church had its own bishop. By the fourth century, congregations of local churches were grouped into dioceses under the

supreme rule of the one bishop, who gradually gained enormous power. During this period the disruption of order in the
Imperial government caused the bishop, as head of an organised community, to be regarded as the sole upholder of order
and security; he assumed the role vacated by the Roman magi-
strate.

The bishops were thought by the Christians in their area to
have almost divine authority. The bishop protected and fed his
people. He appointed the clergy subordinate to him, but also,
and more important, he was, through the apostles, the trans-
mitter of grace to the faithful by his own administration of the
Sacraments and by ordaining the priests who administered
them.

St Paul had regarded the individual *ecclesiae* as members of a
visible community, but he also taught that the 'Universal
Ecclesia' was a Divine Institution – it was the Body of Christ.
This became accepted teaching. The leaders of the Christian
community saw the Christian Church as "The New Israel," a
"Holy Society" governed by the Holy Spirit.

The 'overseers' and 'elders' – now 'bishops' – became rulers
of the local churches and were regarded as the successors of the
apostles, chosen by Christ. The local churches, which were
considered to be of direct Apostolic origin, had a special
prestige and authority, and, among these, Rome, scene of the
martyrdoms of Peter and Paul, had the highest prestige of all.

In 96 AD, Clement, Bishop of Rome, demonstrated how
Rome was already regarded as the leader of the churches. A
group of young Christian men in Corinth, influenced by
Gnostic teaching and practices of asceticism, saw themselves
as a body set apart from other believers by virtue of their
possession of special spiritual gifts. They considered themselves more fit to rule than officially appointed elders. In his
First Epistle to the Corinthians Clement wrote, "...the
Church of Corinth should put aside strife and submit to the
lawfully appointed presbyters, who represent the principle of
divine authority." Clement declared the organisation of

Christian society on earth to be of a hierarchic order under the supreme rule of Christ. He pointed to the Church at Rome as the model for unity, and he showed, by his very intervention in the affairs of the Corinthian Church, that he assumed Rome to have spiritual and juridical authority over the other churches. And this continued to be the general assumption.

When, in 330, Constantinople became Constantine's new capital, the city of Rome lost imperial importance. The Papal Office inherited the political authority abandoned by the imperial government. The Pope filled the role of Emperor in the West and the Roman Church appeared to be the one enduring institution left in the face of encroaching barbarism.

But in the East, the Emperors, especially Constantinus II (who died in 360), were determined to play the leading role in deciding ecclesiastical policy. They carried out their policies through their court bishops, and through the general councils which they invoked. But it seemed natural for Rome, as the Apostolic See, to intervene in the doctrinal debates of these councils, and an appeal to Rome was, as a general rule, regarded as the final appeal. The Western Churches attached less importance than the Eastern to the conciliar system, and looked to the Roman See to maintain their unity.

The Eastern Empire was becoming Europe's centre of culture. The Romans and the Franks were despised as barbarians by the educated Greeks of the East, and it was the growing cultural divergence between East and West that sowed the seeds of the East-West Schism in Christianity. Division began many centuries before the actual Schism in the eleventh century.

The Eastern Church was the centre of doctrinal struggles. In the East, theologians aimed to unite Christian teaching with Greek philosophical culture, in order to incorporate Christian doctrine into a scientific theological system. The West was more concerned with maintaining authentic tradition. From the end of the fourth century, Rome and Constantinople were continuously divided on dogmatic issues, the Arian contro-

versy being the starting point of the divergence. Although the
final schism was to come much later, "...between the fourth
and ninth centuries, the number of years when Rome and
Constantinople were in schism were almost equal to the
number of years when they were in communion." (Christopher Dawson, *Making of Europe*).

Nevertheless, though cultural, political and religious divisions had continued to grow between East and West, the
Christian Empire of the fifth century was still considered to be
Roman and international. Though Roman churchmen no
longer knew Greek and so were isolated from many developments in the East, Latin was still the official language of the
Church. The two halves of the Empire had drifted apart, but
still, in the eyes of Christians, even in the East, a sacred aura
surrounded Rome, giving it special authority. Though Eastern
churchmen outnumbered the Latins at the councils invoked by
the Byzantine Emperors, the ecumenical character of the
councils was recognised, and the Western Church still thought
of itself as the Church of the Empire.

It was mainly due to the strong Popes of the fifth century
that the supremacy of Rome and of the Papacy was finally
established. Pope Damasus had claimed that the Council of
Nicaea in 325 was authoritative only because his predecessor,
Pope Sylvester, had approved it. He, in fact, was the first to
use the Petrine Text to substantiate his case: "And I also say
unto thee, that thou art Peter, and upon this rock I will build
my church; and the gates of hell shall not prevail against it."
(*Mat.* XVI 18). Pope Innocent I, at the start of the next century,
gave practical force to the theological claim by asserting that
no religious question was to be decided without Rome's
cognisance.

Although belief in the Apostolic foundation of the church at
Rome had long been a tradition among the Christians of the
Empire, the doctrine of papal supremacy was only fully developed in the fifth century by Pope Leo the Great. He united the
idea of Rome's civilising mission with the prerogative of the

Apostolic See. But more important, he proclaimed that the Lord had committed to him, as Pope, the care of the whole Church, because he was the heir of St Peter. The doctrine of papal supremacy was then declared in its full sense, using the Petrine Text, and affirming that the faithful should recognise in the Pope the authority of St Peter. The keys of Heaven, he said, were committed to the disciples generally, but to Peter specifically, and therefore Rome had primacy, reaching back through Peter to Christ. As an example of that the Tome, that Pope Leo sent to Chalcedon in 451, was in his view not to be received as a statement for discussion, but as though handed down from St Peter himself; and despite the horrifying squabbles which ensued, the Pope's formulation was eventually accepted as the orthodox teaching of the Church. Furthermore, Leo affirmed that resistance to the Pope's authority involved the mortal sin of pride. Anyone not acknowledging the Roman bishop as head of the Church was not of the body of the Church.

We have now reached the point in history where doctrine declared by the Bishop of Rome to be 'orthodox' was 'orthodoxy'.

At the end of the fifth century, it would seem that, for the majority of Christians, the problems raised and the questions asked since the birth of Christianity could all be quite simply answered: the authentic teachings of Christianity were contained in declarations given from the Holy See. For a thousand years this might well have been the verbal definition of 'orthodoxy'; and though some communities of Christians continued to disagree with each other and to maintain that what they believed contained the truth and that what others believed was heresy, nevertheless there existed a generally established norm.

For the next thousand years, in Western Europe, there was general acceptance of a Universal (or Catholic) Church, with the Bishop of Rome at its head. Many of those today who do not accept a supreme arbiter of doctrine do accept, as part of 'orthodox' Christianity, that there should be an institutional

Church – a body that, as the first bishops held, has the duty of preserving the Scriptures and linking the worship of its present congregation to the original Christian revelation. Christ had said that upon the 'rock' of Peter he would build his *ecclesia* (*Mat.* XVI 18).

But the questioner could still ask – did *ecclesia* mean an organised institution, or did it mean a dedicated group of people? Was there to be a specially instructed school who could impart their secret knowledge to other chosen ones, or was the foundation of a universal, institutional Church the object of Christianity's founder? Was there one known and recognised authoritative body with true continuity; or did true continuity exist within those few unknown, who were real Christians?

How the word 'Church' is understood can affect, and has affected, the form of the questions asked throughout Christianity's history. Above all, it will affect the posing of the difficult question – has Christianity grown in the way its founder intended, and has it kept to its true course?

# XIII

## 'ECCLESIA'

It would appear central to the 'orthodox' Christian's conception of Christianity that Christ came to earth in order to found a universal Church which was to continue for ever, and whose teaching would be for all times, for all places, and for all conditions of men; without the formation of this Church, Christ's coming would have been in vain and, therefore, guarding its continuity must be the most important task in the world.

These ideas were not, of course, clearly formulated for everybody from the beginning, but they formed the background of thought for those who aimed to prevent deviation from what they held to be the true line of tradition. In the second century Irenaeus, who has been called the first great Latin theologian, maintained this view of the Church, and therefore attacked the Gnostics, who did not conceive of Christianity in this way, and who, he feared, could weaken and perhaps even destroy the Great Church itself.

The belief that the creation of a Universal Church – in the sense of a permanent institution – was part of Christ's purpose explains, although it cannot justify, the unchristian actions taken against heretics. It explains how great and good men could be involved in these actions. St Augustine, in the fifth century, as has been seen, finally agreed that force should be used against the Donatists to coerce them back into the main Church. Outside the Church, he said, they would be as a withered limb, and this disunity of Christians would mortally wound the whole Body.

Use of force against heretics was related to national politics.

But even so, the need to safeguard the continuity of the Universal Church was seen to be of such overriding importance that use of force against its 'enemies' was understandable to most religious people.

The Church, itself, as well as having political connection with secular rulers, began to have its own internal politics. These often seem very far removed from the life of the original Christians. Monsignor Ronald Knox has said, "To be a Catholic, it is best not to come too close to the engine room." Nevertheless, as he certainly would have admitted, in order to keep functioning as an institution working in this world, there has to be an engine room. An organisation has to be administered, and the human administrators will be fallible – hence periods of mistakes and even of corruption. But, for those who believe in a Divinely founded Church, Divinely ordained to continue, these errors are not of fundamental importance.

When the word *ecclesia* means the whole body of Christians of every time and place and the institution safeguarding their creed and canon of Scripture – which by the sixth century had become the 'orthodox' meaning – then the questions to be asked are the ones that Cardinal Newman asked: was the Christian Revelation such that the Church was bound to develop the knowledge given? What are the signs of true development? His questions assumed that there is a Divine Plan for a Divine Institution, but ask first, whether the Christian doctrines, as developed and known to Christians of later ages, were unknown to the earliest believers; and, second, what proof have we that they are a legitimate development, arrived at by a continuous and necessary process of definition?

Newman wrote that development was essential; doctrine could not remain in the letter of Scripture – it had to be thought out and formulated. Mysteries, as the word implies, cannot be thought out, but in every Mystery (e.g. the Incarnation, the Resurrection, the Ascension) there are logically comprehensible parts, and these parts can be thought out and, above all, are not contrary to reason. The original Revelation did not answer all questions, and there are many great questions that Scripture alone cannot solve. The Canon of Scripture itself poses a question – does Christianity depend on written documents as does Judaism? Does Scripture need comment, or is it self-interpreting? His arguments led Newman to decided that Scripture needs a final interpreter. "If Christian doctrine admits of true development, it must have an authority provided in the original Dispensation ... Some authority there must be, if there is a Revelation." (Newman, *An Essay on the Development of Christian Doctrine*).

Further, Newman gave as a possible description of the true development of Christianity – as distinct from corruption and variation – the definition of the fifth-century ecclesiastical writer, Vincent of Lerins: "(true) Christianity is what has been held *always, everywhere* and by *all*." But as Newman himself said, such a condition has never existed. The test of legitimate development, for Newman, was whether or not it "retained the essential idea of the subject from which it has proceeded." He argued that large-scale developments exist, professing to be true and legitimate, and "their scale, their antiquity, their gradual but precise formulation" make it appear that their professions are true.

Newman's conclusion is, then, that a development of doctrine is right and necessary; and if there are true developments – and his arguments suggest that there are – then these consist of the doctrines as finally formulated by Popes and Councils. He gives as his reasons, their scale and their longevity, the fact that heretical doctrines contradict each other, that heretical schools split into sects and are often short-lived, that the legitimately developed doctrines have kept their connection with their original idea, and that the world sees these doctrines as one system.

It is possible for many people to accept intellectually that the final formulation of Christian doctrine is a reasonable deduction from the Scriptures known to us. But having studied the complicated and not always edifying processes whereby many of these doctrines reached their final formulation, it becomes clear that only those who hold that the visible Church is a divinely guided body can have any certainty of belief that they have developed truly and faithfully from the original Revelation. But it is also clear that, for Christianity to have continued as a world-religion through the troubled centuries that followed its birth, an organised institution and an established form of dogma were essential. The tendency of human beings to disagree with each other and to commit themselves to opposing beliefs appeared as soon as the new religion took form. Therefore many, who do not necessarily have a firm belief in a divinely instituted Church, would agree that some kind of 'orthodoxy' is necessary to withstand the forces of disintegration.

One of the tasks of 'orthodoxy' is to keep balance. When division between 'orthodoxy' and 'heresy' became centred on formulation of doctrine, a particular kind of balance appeared necessary. It seemed essential that the over-emphasis of any one aspect of the Christian Revelation should be avoided. Such over-emphasis on a single point of doctrine often led to the formation of a heresy, although, in itself, that particular point of doctrine was held by the 'orthodox' to be perfectly valid. This was demonstrated in the theological definitions finally arrived at by the Church councils after the fourth and fifth-century controversies. Christianity was to be neither a rationalised system, whose adherents were simply following the example of a great human teacher, nor a purely mystical religion centred on philosophical myth. In the long and complicated 'orthodox' formulation, accepted at the Council of Chalcedon, Christ was said to be 'True Man and True God'. Theological definitions, of course, cannot give explanations, but they do serve to check exaggerations and to provide a framework within which people are able to interpret their own ideas. Those who try to go beyond repetition of words to find their own meaning in them will inevitably differ from each other. No two minds can think exactly alike. Therefore, every thinking Christian is, to some degree, a 'heretic'. The solid framework of dogma may, surprisingly, allow more freedom for the development of private 'heresies' within it than a vaguer structure can give.

There was also another kind of balance kept by 'orthodoxy'. The Great Church insisted on connecting the Christian Revelation with historical time. This was of fundamental importance. The Gnostics, and all those with a tendency to mysticism, emphasised the Divine and the mythological aspects of Christ. They saw the Christian Revelation in cosmic terms, and they connected it with the highest type of philosophy and philosophical myth known to them. The Church Fathers insisted that Christianity was unique because that which gave rise to the Christian faith had taken place at a specific date in history.

This insistence was vital to the future development of the Christian religion, its rites and its liturgy. It was deeply significant because, as Christianity developed, it could thus be seen as the greatest purveyor of Good News that there had ever been. For the Christian, the ancient myth, common throughout the world, of the sacrifice, death and rebirth of a god, actually happened at a definite time and place on earth, and is being continued today in the celebration of the Eucharist, the main form of worship for all 'orthodox' Christians.

Anchoring the Christian story to historical time helped to prevent psychological and philosophical interpretations evaporating into vague imagery. In many of the Gnostic schools there was a tendency for this to happen, as is seen in some of the later Gnostic writings, when their myths had been elaborated into fantasies. The same tendency can be found in theosophical and kindred groups today. Relation to historical fact helps 'to keep the feet on the ground'.

The heretical groups and schools of the second century understood that special qualities were needed in order to follow the demands for a more inward 'righteousness' than that of 'the Scribes and Pharisees'. But this very understanding sometimes led them to a false sense of their own superiority over the common run of humanity – a danger that has appeared in many such groups throughout the ages. At times, it led, as it has often done, to exclusiveness and even to fanaticism. Again, as with many such groups whose initial teachers may have made valuable discoveries, there formed around them a fringe of exaggeration and sometimes of downright silliness. It was to dangers of this kind that the 'orthodox' were alert and it seems to have been a task of 'orthodoxy' to combat them.

The organised Catholic Church, from its earliest days, has been cautious in its dealings with visionaries and mystics. The guardians of 'orthodoxy' were fearful of a language and a type of teaching that could confuse and lead astray those unable to understand it. They were also fearful of pseudo-mysticism, which was sometimes difficult to disentangle from the true; and it seemed that the passage of time alone made it possible to distinguish the one from the other. They felt that over intensity could lead to wrong emphasis; there was always the danger of concentration on one aspect of Christianity, to the exclusion of others.

The developing Church was, and continued to be, careful for its mass of ordinary church-going members, and careful to keep them from confusion. But though a Church may have been established which endeavoured to keep a balance and that could embrace all manner of people, the adventurers and the enquirers changed and influenced the course of that Church's development, whether part of a plan or no.

"For you are not to suppose, brethren, that heresies could be produced through any little soul. None save great men have been the authors of heresies." (Augustine *Enarrationes in Psalmos* CXXIV). These words were written by St Augustine, himself the most dedicated opponent of heresy and attacker of heretics.

But he also wrote in *De Vera Relig.* VIII, "They (the heretics) are of very great service, not by teaching the truth, of which they are ignorant, but by exciting the carnally-minded Catholics to seek the truth, and the spiritually-minded to disclose it." As we have seen, by their probing and striving for understanding, the heresiarchs caused writers and thinkers in the Great Church to enquire more deeply into their own beliefs. But were the 'spiritually-minded' able to disclose the Truth? Can those who do not understand *ecclesia* as a Divinely appointed Church, be certain that nothing of the original teaching has been lost or distorted in the subsequent history of Christianity? In order to make an idea understandable to all, the idea may have to be, in some way, altered.

# XIV
## 'THE STRONG AND THE WEAK'

Out of the many questions concerning the teachings that became 'orthodoxy' and the teachings that were discarded as 'heresy', the one persistent question emerges again: is there more than one Christianity? It is necessary to make a final return to this question; for it is the question that pervaded most of the first conflicts of belief and encompassed most of the problems which lay within them. It has been shown that the Christian religion was understood, in its earliest days, to be a religion making great demands on those who wished to follow it, and that it took many years of training for a catechumen to be accepted into the body of practising Christians. Even when the rules were relaxed, it was recognised that Christian ethics required a far higher standard of conduct than was the normal custom of the time. The question was then likely to arise: is this religion to be for those who are willing to strive for perfection and have already reached some degree of purity, or is it for everyone, however lax and apathetic?

The existence of different levels of spiritual development among believers was an essential element in the teaching of many early heresies; and in many cases, these different levels showed themselves primarily in what was demanded of each grade of Christian. According to this conception the demands of Christianity were clearly much greater than most people were prepared for, or were able to fulfil. The Marcionites of the second century, and most Gnostic sects, looked on Christian teaching in this way; only the 'Perfect' among the Marcionites were baptised Christians – ordinary 'believers' were only baptised at the time of their death.

Even in the Great Church, it was asked whether, after the forgiveness of sins at Baptism, mortal sins could again be forgiven; and this problem caused many, (for example, Constantine) to postpone their baptism until they were on their death beds, when the fear of sinning was passed.

But the question for the Marcionites and Gnostics also contained a different emphasis. The *ecclesia,* for them, consisted only of those truly prepared to sacrifice themselves, and no one else could enter. Their creation of hierarchical grades among their adherents was influenced by belief in the evil of Matter and therefore in the need for strict asceticism, beyond the capacity of the majority; they also understood that, to fulfil the commandments of Christ, very special effort was needed – effort that the majority was not willing to make.

This same view of *ecclesia* was held by the Donatists in the fourth and fifth centuries. In their eyes, the *ecclesia* was for the strong and faithful only; the cowardly and self-indulgent could not be a part of it.

If Christian teaching were held to be the highest teaching known to mankind, the Donatists had much that was right in their contention. St Augustine himself, said that only saints compose the *true* Church. But he also said that existence on earth implies imperfections – good and bad must grow together within the visible Church of this world. Safeguarding the visible Church of this world was all important to him.

Nevertheless, as has been seen, St Augustine maintained that though mortal man cannot pass judgement on who they are or who they are not, the elect – the élite – are the real Holy Church, the true *ecclesia.* It is on this point that questions arise for those who regard *ecclesia* not as an institution, but as the vehicle for a special teaching, transmitted through those who understand. Can teaching be handed on without distortion? Or – the vital question again – is there more than one Christianity?

Teachers in the Gnostic schools believed that Christ gave secret instruction to his disciples, and they could cite many sayings in the Gospels to bear this out. "And with many such parables spake he the word unto them, as they were able to hear it. But without a parable spake he not unto them; and when they were alone, he expounded all things to his disciples." (*Mark* IV 33, 34).

The important idea running through all heresies based on Gnosticism was the belief that real religions, ancient and contemporary, were connected with one absolute religion. In this religion, the aspiration of the human soul for a life transcending life on earth was the key to the understanding of the universe. The Gnostics held that in all real religions there existed a secret knowledge that could turn this key.

During the centuries immediately before and after the birth of Christianity, there was, throughout the Graeco-Roman Empire, a philosophical movement which strongly influenced religious thinkers, 'orthodox' and 'heretic' alike. The Christian Church was developing during the time that this movement was spreading in most intellectual circles. The movement was known as Neo-Platonism, and it had a close connection with Gnostic ideas.

The manner in which Christian teaching was developed into a theological system owed much to Hellenistic philosophy and language. Many writers of the early Church felt that Plato and those considered to be his followers were close to them in thought; so much so that they sometimes accused the Greek philosophers of borrowing from ancient Jewish and, later, from Christian texts.

The Neo-Platonists perceived that neither sense-perception nor rational cognition were sufficient basis or justification for religious ethics; so they turned away from rationalistic ethics as decidedly as from utilitarian morality. They affirmed that, if man is bound by his psychology – that is to say that, as he is, he cannot go beyond sense-perception and rational cognition in dealing with himself and his surroundings – then he must have a super-human authority to guide him. This implied a philosophy of revelation.

Here the Neo-Platonists were at one with the Christian thinkers. Where they separated from them, and where it seemed to Church leaders that they manifested the dangers also inherent in Gnostic teachings, was in their conception of a perennial, universal religion, centred on the acquisition of true knowledge. The Neo-Platonists held that mankind has an instinctive certainty that there is a supreme goal beyond empirical experience, and yet not an intellectual goal; the Religion, from which all religions have sprung, pointed towards this goal.

The Neo-Platonists never formed an organised religious community. They created, rather, a climate of thought and a way of approach which pervaded religious groups and which stimulated intellectual enquiry. St Augustine tells in his *Confessions* of how the Neo-Platonists helped him to escape from the state of scepticism in which he found himself after his rejection of Manichaeism. He said he owed them much – but, he wrote, Neo-Platonism "only saw afar off the land of its desire". It did not tell him how to get there.

Neo-Platonism had attraction for those with a strong speculative faculty. It certainly had no attraction for the masses. It could be said to be a movement belonging to an élite. St Augustine did not accept an intellectual élite, separate from the ordinary worshippers, but he did believe that there were elect souls chosen by God, who were given grace to work towards perfection, and who formed the true Body of the Church. St Augustine, above all people, believed that Christianity was 'the religion for sinners'. But he also believed that these 'sinners' must recognise themselves as such, and use the means given them to escape from their imprisonment. Those who strove to do this were the chosen souls – the élite. The Gnostics, and the later heretical schools that were influenced by their teaching, were uncompromising in their acceptance of an élite.

Anti-élitism, it must be repeated, is a modern concept. It is a very powerful one today. The notion of 'justice' is now held to imply 'fairness' – and the notion of 'fairness' is held to imply 'equality'.

That there are degrees of excellence in any skill or profession is obvious, and therefore acceptable. But that there are degrees of excellence in behaviour or understanding is not so obvious, and therefore not so acceptable. The idea of a hierarchy of excellence has, in the past, been so corrupted by its arbitrary connection with social power and prestige, that it has become inextricably associated with injustice.

Belief in different levels within humanity was often, in the past, related to belief in previous births or in the pre-existence of souls, and it entered into many ancient religious systems. It entered into the religious teaching of many schools in the early days of Christianity – notably, into those of the Gnostics. In the original Gnostic teaching, the conception of a 'spiritual élite' did not imply privilege, in the sense of 'earthly advantage'. It may have implied 'heavenly advantage', but only in connection with extra demands. "And that servant, which knew his Lord's will, and prepared not himself, neither did according to his will, shall be beaten with many stripes. But he that knew not, and did commit things worthy of stripes, shall be beaten with few stripes." (*Luke* XII 47, 48).

The Gnostics, the Marcionites, the Donatists, in their different ways, believed that there were higher standards expected from "those who knew their Lord's will" than from ordinary people. This, as we saw, led naturally to the question: are there 'two Christianities' – one for the few and one for the 'multitude'?

In Dostoevsky's *Brothers Karamazov*, the Grand Inquisitor says to the Prisoner (Jesus Christ returned to earth), "And if, for the sake of the bread of Heaven, thousands shall follow Thee, what is to become of the millions and tens of thousands of millions of creatures who will not have the strength to forego the earthly bread for the sake of the heavenly? Or dost Thou care only for the tens of thousands of the great and strong, while the millions, numerous as the sands of the sea, who are weak, but love Thee, must exist only for the sake of the great and the strong?" And he goes on, speaking as the voice of the Roman Church, "we are ready to endure the freedom which they (the multitude) have found so dreadful and to rule over them – so awful will it seem to them to be free". Dostoevsky's Grand Inquisitor attacks Christ as the greatest Heretic of all, because he offered a choice, beyond the capability of the millions, whom it was the task of the organised Church to protect.

This fantastic fable in *The Brothers Karamazov* points dramatically to the real problem. How can the masses of the average and the weak fulfil the high demands made by a high religion?

The idea that there are two Christianities is also connected with the idea of different levels of understanding. It is clear that, in popularising scientific theories, certain alterations have to be made in order to simplify them for those not trained in that particular discipline. The same situation may hold for religious teachings. Simplification for mass understanding means some loss and some alteration. A belief in the existence of an original teaching, hidden from those unprepared for it, but taught to those trained in the way to approach it, was maintained by many schools, during the first three Christian centuries.

The theologians of the Great Church, in their fear of the dangers in Gnosticism – dangers which certainly existed, (for example, its tendency towards contempt of this world and of all material things) – turned away from *all* Gnostic ideas. Clement and Origen, Christian teachers in second-century Alexandria, were in touch with Gnostic schools, especially with those of the Valentinians, and they used certain Gnostic ideas in their own teaching. "The true gnostic," Clement wrote, "is the Christian who understands his faith and practises it intelligently." (Clement, *Strom.* 5).

It was central to Clement's ideas that the Christianity of the *pistes,* the ordinary faithful, was valuable and necessary, but that there was also an *inner* teaching leading to knowledge *of* God, not *about* God, and handed down through special teachers, not through ordained Church officials. This teaching could only be understood by those who had been prepared for it.

It has been shown that Origen also laid special emphasis on the different levels within Christian Scripture, and so accepted different levels among Christians. Christ, he said, means different things according to the spiritual progress of the believer; revelation is conditional on the capacity of the recipient; therefore there are different kinds of scriptures, and so of Christian teaching. Origen's term, 'the Flesh of Scripture' as previously explained, is what the masses, (the *pistes*), will understand; and the highest Scripture, 'the Spirit of Scripture' is that in which the stories and events, as given in the Gospels, are understood as vehicles of an inner teaching. These stories and events, though they were actual happenings on earth, are primarily symbols of Christian Revelation. The hidden meanings to which they lead are gradually revealed to those who are attempting to scale the 'heights above mere history' – in his terminology, the 'psychics' and the 'pneumatics', aiming to become the 'perfect' who will have full knowledge.

Nothing is known about the writers of the Gospels. But very early in the history of Christianity it was assumed for certain that, no matter what other books were or were not accepted, the four Gospels were to be read in all Christian communities attached to the Great Church.

Origen showed that the Gospels were written by men possessing a higher understanding than ours and he recognised the layers of meaning contained in them. They were, therefore, not on the same level as the other books and writings which we know.

It is interesting and useful that scholars now examine the Gospels textually, using modern methods of historical research. Much is learnt about the dating and possible alterations or corruptions of text, and about comparison with other literature contemporary with them. But findings are suspect when the researchers treat the Gospels as books on the ordinary level. It can also be worse than this; the Gospels are sometimes regarded as being slightly 'primitive', in the sense of 'uneducated', and lacking the blessings of twentieth-century knowledge. We are accustomed to look on all history from our late twentieth-century position as if from the Day of Judgement, and are unaccustomed to think that, in certain areas, we could have less knowledge than that which belonged to earlier ages.

Origen showed that the Gospel writers purposely wrote the Gospels in the way they did so that people of different levels and possibilities would be able to use them. Perhaps it is here that a clue to the problem of 'two Christianities' can be found.

# XV

# POSSIBILITIES

In a general reading of Church history, a different impression is gained from the Christian controversies of the first three centuries than from those which succeeded them. In those first three centuries, Christian teachers and their schools seem to be searching, in their various ways, for the true meaning of their religion and for the way to practise it. Later, the use of words and logic assumed greater importance. The break-point appears to come at the time when Christianity was accepted as an official religion in the Roman Empire.

Some Christians today hold the view (as did many living at the time) that, when Christianity was recognised as an official religion, it ceased to be Christianity. It became a sign of respectability for those who wanted to advance in the world. It incorporated the legalities of Imperial Rome into its ethics; virtues and vices, punishments and rewards were regulated, as in a legal system. But in the eyes of the 'orthodox', the survival of the Divine Institution through the Dark Ages and the crumbling of civilisation was only made possible by this official recognition and all that it implied. According to this view the administrative organisation of the Church, inherited from the institutions of the Roman Empire, was one of the factors that enabled Christianity to remain a world-religion, instead of dissolving into separate and secret sects.

So we return to the hardest question of all, and the one that most clearly divides the 'orthodox' from those tinged with 'heresy'. Is there a Divine Plan for the growth of Christianity and has Christianity followed that Plan?

The question may be too broad. It involves the whole

theory of a teleological universe. It could include the belief that everything is used to achieve a purpose. A Divine Plan must, by definition, be incomprehensible to human beings. All things judged by us as good or bad may have a purpose unknown to us, though our earth-centred minds tend to think that, if there is a God, He exists for humanity, not humanity for Him.

In the period in which we live, it is difficult to believe in, or to see a sign of, any kind of plan. Our history appears to be one of pointlessness and chaos, and we cannot, in this century, think of it as one of gradual progress upwards, as was the basic assumption of the previous one. The more we study history and the more we learn about the complexities of human nature and the pressures to which it is subject, the changes of climate, the changes of fashion, the impact of economic 'laws' and the movements of opinion and of ideologies, the more we are impelled to equate our known history with chance. The history of Christianity, as we read it, certainly seems to be included in this 'chapter of accidents' – happening bumping against happening. Yet, after centuries of seemingly chaotic human action and reaction, there remains a religious system, which can be recognised as having connection with its beginnings, two thousand years in the past.

Despite centuries of distortion and corruption, the thread that links Christianity to its origins cannot have been completely broken or it would have vanished long ago. The very fact that this organised Christian religion still exists on earth could be a hint of another possibility. People may believe or may not believe in a divinely guided, infallible Church; they may see contradictions arising from human fallibility; they may or may not think that there have been alterations and deviations from an original teaching; but it cannot be denied that there still exists an organised religion, whose committed adherents strive to understand and to comply with what their founder taught, who still keep safe their sacred scriptures and are still connected with their early beginnings – and this through all the unaccountable twists and turns of history.

So our history of chaos may not be the whole story. Many of the Gnostics regarded earthly history as lacking full reality, and subjective, because seen through mortal eyes. Related only to itself, it is a jumble of happenings, meaning nothing. To the Gnostics the truths of religious knowledge which they sought were part of objective history or, as they termed it, supra-mundane history. Supra-mundane history was, in Gnostic teaching, the history of Reality and, for human beings, only understandable in terms of myth.

Like the Gnostics, Origen taught that the purpose of life was the return of the divine spark within mankind to its Source. For him the historic events in Christian teaching were the time-space appearance of a supra-temporal cosmic plan. In this he was close to St Paul, whom some Gnostic schools regarded as their founder. Origen likened the history that we learn to a ladder, the first steps of which are time-and-space happenings. The understanding of these leads upward to awareness of the Mysteries at the heart of the universe. According to Origen's system, there is a history of another order than ours – the supra-mundane order – and this history may sometimes connect with ours in earthly time. So following Origen's ideas, the Christian Mysteries may have been glimpses in our world of this objective order, this Divine Plan, although the meaning of these glimpses still lies far beyond our comprehension.

It has been said that many of the divisions between 'orthodox' and 'heretic' arose through their continuing attempts 'to express the inexpressible'. Words hold danger. Founders of heresies sometimes made spiritual discoveries; they gained a particular insight, or understood an idea in a new way; they then wrote or preached about it, and then the discovery strayed from the mark. It was often the attempt to solve problems lying beyond logic and sense-perception that led to the 'unbalance of heresy'.

Disagreements about language have often been treated as if they were disagreements about what is or is not objective truth. Since theology deals with the Infinite, there can hardly be a theological statement that is not an analogy. The danger arises for theologians when this fact is overlooked, as it commonly has been. For Christian theologians the truth is that which Christ revealed, so that the 'analogous' statements of the theologians have value for Christians in so far as they approach the original Revelation.

In Judaism and in Christianity God is spoken of in anthropomorphic terms – as when He is described as being 'angry' or being 'pleased', in the same way as human beings are. The mistake of anthropomorphism lies less in thinking and speaking of God in human terms – because the construction of our minds leads us to do this – than in forgetting that we are then using analogies.

The simple believers in both Judaism and Christianity, have long used this natural way of thinking to aid their belief. It may not be quite the same for the more intellectual Christian and the theologian, who could be tempted to treat anthropomorphic expressions as if they actually defined the relation of God to man. By treating these expressions as descriptions of fact, it can be made to seem that Truth has been reached, when it is still being pursued.

The same danger arises in regard to the logical formulation of doctrine. The definitions finally reached by the Church councils after long and arduous struggle have value in their rejection of exaggeration and in their formation of a framework for thought. But logical definitions of doctrine are a beginning rather than an end. For the 'orthodox', as well as for the 'heretic', there is always more to be understood – the Truth has still to be sought. What seems to be certain is that an easily explained, moralistic religion, rational and totally comprehensible, could not have had the sudden and powerful impact which the Christian religion had at its birth, nor could it have endured all the horrors of history for two thousand years.

We cannot find the answers to religious mysteries through mere intellectual puzzling. It is impossible to make a real study of a religion without trying to practise it. "A man does not

merely *think* his religion and feel it, he 'lives' his religion as
much as he is able, otherwise it is not religion but fantasy or
'philosophy'." (P.D. Ouspensky, *In Search of the Miraculous*)
But, in order to 'live' a religion, people must, of course, try to
understand it to the limit of their powers.

Clement and Origen used whatever seemed of value to
them in the ideas of Gnosticism in order to further their
understanding. The inner connection between religions and
between religious myths, particularly those of ancient times,
formed an important part of Gnosticism. This was accepted by
the two Alexandrian teachers, but was an idea that the 'orthodox' Church generally disregarded. The Church apologists, in
their distrust of the Gnostics' influence and in their dislike of
the Gnostics' often foolish extravagances, may have lost hints
that could have helped them in the unravelling of their great
problems.

Our knowledge of the Gnostics is limited, and it is difficult
to be certain how much they invented and how much they
learnt from older traditions. But Clement and Origen formed
a connecting bridge between them and the Christian Church,
and lent balance to their views.

Clement and Origen are not now considered to be 'heretics',
but neither are they strictly 'orthodox'. It has been said that, in
the first centuries, when the Christian religion was still in the
state of formation, the great Gnostic teachers did not leave the
Christian 'main road' (for the main road did not then exist),
but that this 'road' took another direction from theirs. (cf.
F.C. Burkitt, *Church and Gnosis*).

The 'road' might have been constructed differently had it
led over Clement's and Origen's 'bridge' – that is to say, had
the Alexandrians' writings been followed more closely as
'orthodox' teachings. The Western Church has long laid stress
on the Christian's duty of obedience to Church discipline.
More fundamentally, it has stressed duty to fellow human
beings; and from this teaching, European civilisation has
gained such benefit that, though Christendom may no longer

exist, the Christian ethic remains. Eastern religions have put more emphasis on practices leading to self-knowledge and to interior spiritual growth. It is possible that, had Clement's and Origen's teachings been originally accepted into mainstream Christianity, there would have been a greater emphasis laid on the inner and mystical understanding of religion, which many now feel they must go to the East to rediscover.

The 'orthodox' institutional Church has formulated dogmas that are accepted, to a greater or a lesser degree, by millions of diverse human beings. Through twenty centuries an ethical standard has been more or less accepted as a recognised ideal. This is the Christianity guarded by the 'orthodox' for the sake of the millions.

In the last analysis, it might seem that provision has been made for the 'pistes'; but that for the 'psychics' and for the 'pneumatics' it has been more difficult. It took a long time for Meister Eckhart, philosopher-mystic of the fourteenth century, and for St John of the Cross, the great Mystic and Saint of the sixteenth, to achieve recognition. But, if 'orthodoxy' had not guarded the institutional Church from destruction and had not affirmed and preserved its dogmas, there might have been no solid base from which the searchers could search. Both high and low are able, in their different ways, to go on searching within what has been given and in their different ways, to explore what lies beyond the 'chapter of accidents'.

The beginning of philosophy, Clement quotes Plato as saying, is found in the attitude of wonder. Clement connected this attitude with a saying in the *Gospel of Hebrews,* (a document which he apparently used, but which is now lost): "He who seeks will not cease until he finds; when he finds, he will be astonished; when he is astonished, he will reign; when he reigns, he will rest." (R.M. Grant, quoted in *Secret Sayings of Jesus*).

In this saying, Clement has summed up the aim of a religious being. The definition here of a religious being is not one who adopts a religious label and assumes that this gives the answers to all problems; it is rather one who is not content with words, nor with the life of sense-experience alone, but is aware of something within and beyond, and of the need to reach it.

Clement saw wonder as the beginning of the search for holiness (wholeness), then the need to ponder and to continue to ponder – to wonder and to ponder, two activities of Clement's Christian gnostic. "And Mary kept all these things and pondered them in her heart." (*Luke* II 19).

The birth and growth of Christianity are still shrouded in mystery. Perhaps the important thing is to recognise that they *are* a mystery. It has not been explained how, against all the odds, and surviving all the pressures that would normally destroy an institution, organised Christianity, as a world religion, still exists; the very fact that questions concerning its birth and growth are still unresolved may even be a clue.

Nothing can be taken for granted. The doctrines of Christianity have achieved formulation, but intellectual knowledge of 'orthodox' doctrine does not mean 'knowledge' in the gnostic sense – the meaning in St John's Gospel. Very long search is needed for the acquisition of that.

In Christian churches every Sunday, truly astonishing statements are made, and they have been made so often that people do not notice how extraordinary they are. No matter how many doctrines have been formulated, it is still necessary for each person to discover what they mean for him or herself and to enter into their meaning.

The first step on Origen's ladder to the Mysteries may, perhaps, be found here, where the many questions unite – is there a hidden Christianity that exists, and has always existed, within the Christianity accessible to all? It is said many times in the Gospels that only he who has ears to hear will hear. It is also true that only those "who hunger and thirst" will find answers.

# BIBLIOGRAPHY

Angus, S, *Religious Quests of the Greek and Roman World*, Cambridge University Press, 1967.

Baur, Walter, *Orthodoxy and Heresy in Earliest Christianity*, Philadelphia Fortress Press, 1971.

Bigg, Charles, *The Christian Platonists of Alexandria*, 2nd edition, 1913.

Burkitt, F C, *Church and Gnosis. A Study of Christian Thought and Speculation in the Second Century. The Morse Letters* for 1931, Cambridge, 1932, reprinted 1978.

Burrows, Millar, *The Dead Sea Scrolls*, New York, The Viking Press, 1955.

Carrington, P, *The Early Christian Church*, Cambridge University Press, 1957.

Chadwick, H, *The Early Church*, Pelican History of the Church, Penguin, 1967.

Daniélou, J & Marrou, H I, *The Christian Centuries. The First Six Hundred Years*, Darton, Longman & Todd, reprinted 1964.

Daniel-Rops, H, *The Church in the Dark Ages*, London, J M Dent & Sons, 1959.

Dawson, Christopher, *The Making of Europe*, London, Sheed & Ward, 1946.

Dodd, C H, *Interpretation of the Fourth Gospel*, Cambridge University Press, 1953.

Grant, R M & Freedman, D N, *The Secret Sayings of Jesus*, London, Fontana, 1960.

Kung, Hans, *On Being a Christian*, London, Collins Fount, 1978.

Ladure, E Le Roy, *Montaillou*, Scolar Press, 1978.

Manschrek, C L, *A Study of Christianity in the World. From Persecution to Uncertainty*, New Jersey, Prentice Hall Inc., 1974.

Newman, John Henry, *An Essay on the Development of Christian Doctrine*, 1845 Edition, Pelican Classic, 1974.

Nicoll, Maurice, *The Mark*, London, Watkins Publishers, 1954.

Ouspensky, P D, *A New Model of the Universe*, London, Kegan Paul, 1938.

Ouspensky, P D, *In Search of the Miraculous*, New York, Harcourt Brace, 1949.

Przywara, E, *An Augustine Synthesis*, London, Sheed & Ward, 1945.

Robinson, James (Ed.), *Nag Hammadi Library in English*, San Francisco, Harper & Row, 1978.

Wiles, M, *Making of Christian Doctrine*, Cambridge University Press, 1967.

Wilson, E, *Scrolls from the Dead Sea*, London, W H Allen, 1955.

Yamauchi, E M, *Pre-Christian Gnosticism*, Tyndale Press, 1973.

# INDEX

Index 157